UNTIL DEATH DO US PART

Rev. Darlene,

God bless you for all that you do for God's Glory!

May you be strengthened and encouraged as you read my first book.

Rev. Dr. Mary White Williams
(Rev. Mary)
6/25/2015

UNTIL DEATH DO US PART

DR. MARY WHITE WILLIAMS

Copyright © 2015 by Dr. Mary White Williams.

Library of Congress Control Number: 2015906134
ISBN: Hardcover   978-1-5035-6311-7
               Softcover   978-1-5035-6312-4
               eBook   978-1-5035-6313-1

All rights reserved. No part of this book may be reproduced or transmitted in any form or by any means, electronic or mechanical, including photocopying, recording, or by any information storage and retrieval system, without permission in writing from the copyright owner.

Any people depicted in stock imagery provided by Thinkstock are models, and such images are being used for illustrative purposes only.
Certain stock imagery © Thinkstock.

Print information available on the last page.

Scripture quotations marked NKJV are taken from the New King James Version, copyright © 1982 by *Thomas Nelson Inc.* Used by permission. All rights reserved.

Rev. date: 05/11/2015

To order additional copies of this book, contact:
Xlibris
1-888-795-4274
www.Xlibris.com
Orders@Xlibris.com
701365

CONTENTS

1. From the Beginning (Ohanio/Mary) 1
2. The Inevitable 21
3. A Time of Preparation 33
4. Wedding/Honeymoon 51
5. The Reaffirmation of Vows 63
6. Leaving, Cleaving, and Becoming One Flesh 67
7. What Is Marriage? 79
8. Marriage Is a Learning Experience 87
9. Communication Is Key 97
10. Some of Our Sayings and Scriptures 107
11. Complimenting Made Easy 115
12. What about Children? 125
13. The Myth of "Playing House" 135
14. The Glamour Has Gone 145
15. What Is Love? 153

Foreword

UNTIL DEATH DO US PART

By Dr. Mary White Williams

In the narrative of scripture found in II Kings 22: 14-20 and II Chronicles 34:22-23, the book of the law is found in the temple by the high priest Hilkiah, during the reign of Josiah. Upon discovery of this book, the wisdom of the prophetess Huldah was sought. Huldah was a married woman who lived in Jerusalem and based upon her translation of the word of God the famous Judaic reform under Josiah was begun. The discovery of the book of the law was a major breakthrough in the life of the nation and yet no action was taken until the revered and trusted woman of God whose name was Huldah rendered her interpretation and gave instruction from the word of God. In an era and culture when women for the most part were seldom consulted or heeded, Huldah emerged, as did several other exceptional biblical women, as a revered and indispensable voice of wisdom whose counsel was considered indispensable for the future of the kingdom.

Dr. Mary White Williams, woman of God, wife, preacher, prayer warrior and intercessor, pastor, homemaker, educator and author, embodies the spirit, character, integrity and heart for God as the biblical Huldah. She walks in all of her roles and discharges all of her duties with competence and commitment, with passion and power, with responsibility and respect, and with honor and holiness. I formally met Dr.

Williams and her husband when I was assigned as pastor of St. James African Methodist Episcopal Church in Newark, New Jersey in 1984. At that time she was a member of the pulpit staff of that great historic congregation. After serving with me for a number of years she felt called to be a pastor. She started a congregation in one of the roughest parts of Newark and served that congregation with distinction until she was promoted to a larger church where she continued to make full proof of her ministry.

Throughout the years all of the members of the Watley household family have been blessed to know Dr. Williams as a woman of God, we have appreciated her generous and caring spirit as well as her sincere and heartfelt prayer life. She is one of those rare individuals who continue to grow and seek new vistas in ministry, in life and in her devoted walk with God. I am sure that her insights and reflections in this book will enhance the lives of all of those who are privileged to partake of its contents. Dr. Williams walks her talk and those of us who have known her down through the years, await with anticipation and expectation the next incarnation and manifestation of her ever expanding vision, ministry and witness to the gospel of the Lord Jesus Christ.

William D. Watley,
Epiphany, 2015

Guest Foreword

"Until death do us part" are very strong words. Not only are they uttered in a marriage ceremony, but it is also a reality for those who have decided to fulfill the commitment.

Dr. Mary White-Williams has fulfilled those very words with her husband Pastor Ohanio Williams. The love that was displayed was that of a love depicted for us as demonstrated in Christ's love for the Church.

The courtship of Pastor Williams and Dr. Mary was indeed special. Not only did both have a constant desire to serve and honor the Lord, but both demonstrated this behavior prior to marriage, and continued this after the vows were voiced.

In today's society, (unfortunately) the up and coming generations do not have an example of being involved in a Godly relationship; courtship or marriage. Our reality produces evidence that the divorce rate amongst Christians is at an alarmingly high percentage. Is it by chance that there *is a lack of marriage mentors* available to show this generation the biblical way?

While reading *"Until Death do us part"* the reader will get a wonderful synopsis of what a Godly union resembles and should possibly emulate for Godly success overall.

For Dr. Mary Williams and Pastor Ohanio, mutual love and respect has been the theme of *their* marriage. The ability to work as a team was vital to the success of their relationship; recognizing that the Lord is present in every conversation and decision. The word of God shows us several examples of a marriage. The first marriage documented in the Bible gives examples of the roles and responsibilities that each should act in. When these roles are deviated from, resentment can take place. Commitment to the relationship and each other, are vital for success. If either party feels taken for granted or even used, that is the recipe for destruction.

In this book, scripture is used as a foundation. Each stage of the relationship is outlined to assist the reader if they have any pending questions.

Written from the perspective of life learning experiences, Dr. Williams provides true examples of the process so that each reader can conceptualize the scenario. A guide for those who are interested in courtship, marital life and Godly relationships, *"Until death do us part"* can be used as a practical tool for those who are serious about taking their relationship to the next level.

Congratulations, to Dr. Mary White-Williams, for fulfilling her desire to document her life experience, as it reflects the words that she has lived with Pastor Ohanio Williams; "Until death do us part".

Claudia G. Barnett, PhD
Training and Performance Improvement Technologist
Doctoral Mentor
Author: The Dissertation Process: A Step by Step Mentored Guide

Dedication

To the Creator of the universe and the one who instituted marriage, thank you for teaching me how to be the wife that Ohanio loved and cherished for thirty-three years.

This book is dedicated to the life and memory of Rev. Ohanio Alexander Williams, who was the "love of my life." Our marriage, I do believe, was God-ordained. Time and place were not barriers or hindrances, for the Lord brought Ohanio all the way from St. Croix, US Virgin Islands, in search of a better life, and we believed that a part of that better life was to find me. Proverbs 18:22 was quoted by Ohanio often, "He who finds a wife finds a good thing. And obtains favor from the LORD." Ohanio did find a better life; it had to be of God, for who else could have allowed Ohanio to declare so boldly on our first meeting, "In the presence of the Lord, there is fullness of joy, and at your right hand, there are pleasures forevermore, but she is at my left hand."

I do remember the place and the moment that those words were spoken, and the rest is history. The title of this book was born out of our declaration to each other; this is *Until Death Do Us Part*!

Thank you, Lord, for letting Ohanio find me. For thirty-three years, You allowed us to love each other with mutual respect, and You nudged him often to remind me that I was the best thing that ever happened to him and to say to me, "If I had to get married again, I would get married to you."

To all the single, unmarried persons, my desire for you is that your dream of finding your future partner will become a reality.

To all who are married, I pray that as you apply the principles laid out in this book, you will experience greater fulfillment as the Creator intended.

Acknowledgments

Above all others, I give God the glory for allowing me the opportunity, step by step, to complete this project. Time and space will not allow me to name the numerous individuals who have poured into my life and ministry and have encouraged me. Some have gone from "labor to reward," and I cherish their memory.

For those who have prayed for me daily, you know who you are, and I say, "Thank you!"

To my mom and dad, Henry White Jr. and Nancy Page White, who always believed in me; I will always bless your memory. Thank you for giving me life and encouragement.

To the memory of my brothers: William, Henry, Roland, and Lonzer White. I am grateful for the life we shared.

To my only sister, Elaine White. You pray for me every day and for the success of this book. I love you.

To all my relatives, thank you for your faith in me, your love and respect for me, and your desire to see my first book published. I am grateful that we are a supportive family.

To my prayer partners and all who encircle me in prayer daily, I say, "Thank you!"

To Overseer Elnora Pratt and Rev. Gena Johnson. Thank you for being a part of our lives for so many years. We have ministered and served together. You have always had a servant's spirit, even serving food at our wedding. You are so special.

To Rev. Geraldine K. Branch. Thank you for your prayers, prophetic words, and always being available to me. Thank you also for serving as vice president of the Mary White Williams Ministries, Inc. after Ohanio's passing.

To Sister Phyllis Tait. I am thankful for your knowledge in so many areas. Thank you for your prayers and encouragement, especially for this book. Thank you, Dr. Claudia B. Barnett, for your encouragement and prayers during this project. A special "thank-you" to Doctors Alonzo and Sandra Gay and Acts Ministry. You encouraged me greatly and have declared that there is a special anointing on my life and this book. Again, thank you!

To Evangelist Shirley Johnson. Thank you for your prayers, encouragement, friendship, and for being a very special sister in Christ.

To Bishop William H. Henderson and Rev. Dianna Henderson. Thank you for your love, your prayers, your friendship through the years, and your prayers for this book. I love you.

To Pastor Slaughter and my St. James AME Church family in Newark, New Jersey. Thank you for your prayers and the many opportunities to serve.

To Dr. William D. Watley, my colleague and friend. Thank you for taking time out of your busy schedule to write the foreword for my first book.

To the life, ministry, and memory of my friend and sister in Christ, Rev. Dr. Annabelle Freeland—Dr. Freeland and I traveled in the United States and abroad for many years. She had a great passion for missions and education; she was a great friend to me and Ohanio.

To all of our godchildren and spiritual children who were born into the kingdom of God because of our ministry: "Keep on keeping on." Thank you!

To Brother Bogg and Sister Regina Johnson. Thank you for being constant and faithful through all these years. Whenever I need your assistance, day or night, you are always available. You are truly a lasting fruit.

To our daughters who are in ministry:

Rev. Dr. Deborah K. Blanks, Assistant Dean of Religious Life at Princeton University, Princeton, New Jersey. We love you and have always been proud of your accomplishments.

Rev. Teresa Lynn Rushdan, the pastor of Bethel AME Church in Madison, New Jersey, may the Lord always bless you and Desirée as you continue to preach the truth of the gospel.

To Mrs. Elaine Blancks O'Neill, who was in the first class (third grade) that I taught at Washington School in Rutherford, New Jersey. Thank you for being a prayer partner, using your many musical talents, puppetry, and so much more. Thank you for assisting me in the ministry with all of your gifts and talents.

To the Vauxhall Branch Library Staff. The manager, Erica Bell, Tracy Franklin, Saundra Miller, Roberta Chambers, Peter De Matteo, Laterria Sims, Ambria Askew, Taria Bryan, and Kurt Carter—thank you for providing a safe and comfortable place for me to work on my project. To all the children and adults who opened the door and did other deeds of kindness as I am in and out of the library regularly, thank you!

To Mr. Robert Bowers and others who drove me to the library and other appointments. I thank God for you.

To Dr. Alfred B. Johnson, who shared insights from his ministry as "The Village Pastor," in his first publication with Xlibris Corporation, and he recommended them to me.

To Tiffany Minott. Thank you for selecting this picture as a "classic" for the cover of the book.

To Ella Thompson, president of ET Printing Press, who accepted the challenge to type my manuscript. My prayer is that you were strengthened and encouraged as you typed. May your dreams be realized.

To Phyllis Ossai. Thank you taking pictures of my engagement and wedding rings and then, forwarding all of the images to Xlibris. Your expertise has been invaluable.

Introduction

There are many people who no longer believe in the sanctity of the marriage bond or the traditional wedding ceremony. Some have said that going through a wedding ceremony is a waste of time—why bother? Why go through the hassle of getting a marriage license or a blood test?

I have an answer for all of those who may think those thoughts, or who may dare to ask those questions. First of all, you cannot drive a car, fly an airplane, or go hunting or fishing without a license. Getting a license allows an individual the privilege, the right, and the legal permission to do something. Living together without legal documentation is settling for less than God's best for you. In fact, it is an offense to God.

"Common-law" marriage or "shacking," although widely practiced and accepted in some states, is not a marriage in the sight of God. What it really is, is two people coming together—cohabiting without legal documentation. God's desire is for all of us to live happy and satisfied lives whether we choose to marry or remain single.

In marriage, a couple can live together without guilt, thus honoring God. Hebrews 13:4 says, "Let marriage be held in honor (esteemed worthy, precious, of great price, and especially dear) in all things. And thus let the marriage bed be undefiled (kept undishonored), for God will judge and punish the unchaste [all guilty of sexual vice] and adulterous" (The Amplified Bible).

Until Death Do Us Part was written as a guide for all who are satisfied in their singleness, for those who are believing God for that special person, and for those who desire a more fulfilling marriage.

From the Beginning

Ohanio

Ohanio Alexander Williams was born on Saturday, December 25, 1926. What a wonderful Christmas present for Christian Williams and Mildred Miller, and the setting was the breathtaking Frederiksted, St. Croix, US Virgin Islands. St. Croix has lovely beaches with white sand.

Ohanio was an unusual child. He was playful, serious, and hardworking; and he enjoyed helping. He learned how to work without complaining. Ohanio's parents and grandparents were poor farmers who lived on the land and were sustained by the land. Because Ohanio was smart and wise for his age, he learned how to fit in and how to manage in all kinds of situations.

When Ohanio was eight years old, his mother died in childbirth; and his sister, a little girl, also died. Ohanio told me that he was the one who told the nurse that his mother was not moving. The experience was painful for him then, and even as he told me about it, the hospital scene was still very vivid to him. Even though he was very close to his maternal grandmother, he became more attached to her after the death of his mother. He fondly called her Granny. Granny loved her grandson, and her nickname for him was "Hano."

Ohanio grew up as an only child. Ohanio loved his dad very much, and he was very happy and proud when people mentioned how much they looked alike. They did look alike, except for the age difference. His dad left the island in search of a brighter and better future. Christian Williams relocated to New York City. There he married Miriam. Ohanio was "crushed" when his dad left him. There is an old adage that says, "When life hands you lemons, make lemonade."

Even though Ohanio was young, he was very strong physically and mentally. Life has a way of maturing you, helping you to do whatever is necessary for survival. He learned how to carry water on his head. Ohanio referred to this activity as "carting water." Most of the "islanders"—that I have observed have excellent postures. They walk tall and straight, and so did Ohanio.

Because there was no running water in the house, Ohanio had to keep the barrel filled. He got up early in the morning, before school, and "carted water." After school, he did the same. Most of the time, he wore no shoes. He learned at an early age how to do without or get along on very little with a thankful heart. Ohanio was serious-minded and did not take anything for granted. In reminiscing, he often talked about the times when it was important to dress for some special occasion, and he did not have the suit or some other proper clothes to wear. There were times when a family member or a friend died, and Ohanio inherited their clothing. Often, his thoughts were, *When I grow up, things will be different. I will have nice clothes to wear. I will have shoes to put on my feet. I won't have to wear* "hand-me-downs" or wait until someone dies to "look nice."

During his growing-up years, it was his grandmother, Mathilda Miller, who helped to mold him and to assure him that God was going to bless him. Ohanio and Granny worked as a team. Granny was a strong, statuesque, hardworking tall woman. She was also very independent and an excellent cook. They worked hard all week. Granny then prepared special dishes and, with the help of her grandson, gathered other saleable items, and they went to "the market" on Saturday, hoping to make a good profit.

Beatrice Johnson was close to his grandmother. He told me about the number of times that she "saved his skin" from getting a whipping. He may have forgotten a chore or knocked over the milk. Ohanio was not clumsy, but from time to time, as children do, he was into mischief. I remember meeting Beatrice Johnson; she seemed bigger than life because of all the stories I had heard about her. She had a great smile, and she made you feel "at ease" and "at home." Because she loved

"Hano," she could not do enough for his wife. She really was excited about meeting me (on my first trip to St. Croix.) She prepared special meals for me. I remember that on one of the visits, she made "johnnycakes" and guava candy. There were so many other treats and gifts that I received, and at no time did I feel like an outsider. I have heard it said "that one who would have friends must show himself or herself to be friendly."

Ohanio grew up in Frederiksted, St. Croix, US Virgin Islands, and attended St. Patrick Catholic Church. He was an "altar boy" for many years; in some of our churches, he would be called an acolyte. Other members of his family were also faithful members of St. Patrick Catholic Church, including his cousin, Alma.

Cousin Alma Doward was from Whim Estate and was a very powerful influence in Ohanio's life. He spoke of her often and with great affection. Years later, when I met her, we connected instantly. The "chemistry" was there. She called me Niecey. To her, I was special. There was a sour sap (a native fruit) tree in front of her house. From that tree, she picked sour saps, pounded them, and then made me a delicious cool drink. She did so many endearing things for me on every visit. Cousin Alma was also an excellent cook.

Eglantine Weeks (Dully), one of her daughters, was a great friend and cousin to Ohanio. They were "buddies." There were times when they got into mischief together. Dully married James Weeks; it is said that we all have a twin somewhere. Ossie Davis was definitely that look-alike. On many of our visits, we stayed with Dully and James, and today, I am the beneficiary of their closeness, and I am also close to the other members of the Doward family.

Ohanio spoke of "Foster Gate." "Foster," as he referred to it, was where everything happened—all the news, etc. Ohanio lived in the "Foster" area. After I heard Ohanio tell some of the tales of "Foster," I had a certain picture in my mind. The people in that community gathered there, mostly in the evenings, to greet each other and to chat and find out the latest happenings of the day.

The way Ohanio spoke about "Foster Gate," I was expecting a gate or entranceway of special significance. What I found was a water fountain: an ordinary water fountain. At different times in our lives, things and places take on a special meaning. There are places that I remember when I was a child. At the time, the place seemed very large, but years later, it was somehow different from what I remembered.

To Ohanio and the people of "Foster," I am sure that they had great and memorable times together. To them, "Foster Gate" was the head of the town. Since "Foster Gate" was a very special part of Ohanio's life, I often try to capture those days when he was happy meeting with family and friends, as they shared the news of the day. There was never sadness or regret when Ohanio told me about various episodes and escapades that happened in "Foster." After graduating from Christiansted High School, Ohanio worked for a short time at the army base. He had the desire to become a pharmacist. He expressed this to his father. Even though Ohanio loved

Granny, he wanted to be reunited with his father, and his father did promise to help him get a better education. His dad sent for him, and Ohanio was very excited. He did not want to leave Granny, but he also had the dream of greater things in New York. When he arrived in New York, there was no talk about him becoming a pharmacist or his father helping him. When Ohanio was leaving home, Granny told him, "Don't leave home a 'johnnycake' and come back a dumpling!" Ohanio was determined to succeed.

Once again, Ohanio learned how to "take lemons and make lemonade." He moved in with his father and stepmother, Miriam. He immediately found a job as an errand boy and went to school at night to become a printer. He paid rent to his father and saved a little money whenever possible. When his father told him that he was going to take him to the bank to open up an account, how surprised his father was when Ohanio showed him his bankbook.

Ohanio had the tenacity of a "bulldog." He told me about his difficulty when he tried to get into printing school in New York. Even though Ohanio was told that there was no space for him, he did not take no for a final answer. He waited until the class was over and went up to the instructor. These were the words that he spoke, "I noticed a few students reading the 'funnies,' and they were not really paying attention to what you were trying to teach. They are just taking up space, and I want to learn about printing." Because of Ohanio's persistence, the instructor invited him to attend the next class session. He was an excellent student who worked during the day and attended classes in the evening. He memorized scripture verses and often quoted God's promises—for example, "I can do all things through Christ which strengthens me" (Phil. 4:13).

Ohanio worked at the Print Shop in New York. He began as an "errand boy." His boss told him that in the first opportunity he had, he would put him on the printing press. Ohanio held on to what he heard. On his regular job and in school, God gave him favor. He worked on the printing press, and he stayed at the Print Shop for twenty-three years.

In his poem "Street Sweeper," Dr. Martin Luther King Jr. admonishes us to strive for excellence. In the poem, he lifts up Michelangelo, who painted; Beethoven, who composed music; and Shakespeare, who wrote poetry. They all excelled in their individual fields.

Whatever Ohanio did, he put his whole heart into it. During his years at the Print Shop, Ohanio was punctual, dependable, and well respected. Whenever there was a money transaction, he could be trusted to take the money to the designated place, and there was never any problem. Being the person—the man he was—proved to be a blessing to both of us years later.

Ohanio accepted the Lord as his personal Savior at Bethel Gospel Tabernacle in Jamaica, New York, before I met him. He also attended Bethel Bible Institute right there at the church. He was a faithful tither, an excellent student, and a "soul winner." The late Bishop Roderick R. Caesar Sr. was his pastor, his "father in ministry," and his mentor.

Bishop Caesar was a precious, humble, soft-spoken servant of the Lord, and much of the wisdom that Ohanio possessed, I do believe, came from Bishop Caesar. By the time I met Ohanio, it was already "drilled" into him that marriage is not "fifty-fifty" but "100%-100 %"! Bishop Caesar prepared him for marriage by telling him, "If you live to love her and she lives to love you, you will be happy and have a successful marriage."

When Ohanio first saw me, it was probably "love at first sight," and he was prepared and ready to get married as a lifetime commitment. As I mentioned earlier, Ohanio came from a humble background. Very often, we misjudge people, and we don't have a clue to their background, why they do what they do or dress in a certain way. Ohanio always believed that God would allow him to have a better life than what he knew as a young boy. He had a grateful heart for the small things in life. He was never wasteful and was always looking for ways to bless the hungry and needy.

Mary

Henry White Jr. and Nancy Page White were my parents. My oldest brother was William; then Henry was born. My mom told me that after the two boys were born, she wanted a girl. I was that girl. My mom already had the name in her mind, Mary, with the middle name Lou. Within the next year, Roland was born, then about a year later, Lonzer (Lonnie), and two years later, Elaine was born—six children in all, and we were all born in Newark, New Jersey. The "high-rise" apartments were not a part of my culture; we lived in tenement apartment buildings. Most of the apartment buildings had front apartments and back apartments. You paid more for the front view.

My preschool years were spent on Elm Street. Then the family moved to Monmouth Street, and the grammar school years were spent on Charlton Street. There was excitement and activity all around us. Most of the food that we ate could be purchased from the stores right in our block or in our neighborhood.

I was born before air conditioners and, certainly, before televisions. When it was hot, we opened the windows and put screens in them to keep the flies and other bugs out of our apartment. Later, we used fans to cool the rooms.

To keep the food cold and to keep it from spoiling, we ordered ice from the "iceman." The block of ice was placed in the icebox, of course; a pan was placed under the icebox to catch the water as the ice melted. The "coolerator" was the next invention; it looked better than the icebox, but a pan still had to be placed under it to catch the melted water.

When it was too hot to sleep, my parents and all the children would come downstairs and sit on the "stoop." (The "stoop" consisted of steps that were the entranceway into the building.) Most of our neighbors did the same. We had great fun. We played hopscotch, jacks, checkers, hide-and-seek, and of course, we were good at jump rope. You might be thinking, *It was night and dark. How could they see?* Our street, Charlton Street, was well lit! We were happy, and I still have good memories of those times.

We lived before what some call "the projects." Our buildings were called tenement apartments. There were no gangs like the ones that are feared today. Most of the time, you did not have to worry about locking your door. We were poor but had many happy times together as a family.

My mom was a great cook. She made everything from scratch. She really did wonders in the kitchen. We enjoyed nourishing hot meals every day. Since Charlton Street School was right down the street from our house, we came home for lunch. On Sundays, we could be assured of delicious fried chicken, rice with brown gravy, possibly string beans or collard greens, and of course, cake and Jell-O. Whoever heard of anybody making white potato pies with meringue on the top! On a regular basis, my mom made big tea cookies. There was "good eating" at our house, and our friends enjoyed eating with us. Our house was like the "house by the side of the road."

Graduations were held twice a year—at the end of January and at the end of June. During my teenage years (in the summer time), I found ways to earn extra money; I have always liked having my own money. One of my summer jobs included working at the Empire Pickle Factory on Boyd Street, and while working there, I learned how to cap jars of pickles and pickle products as they moved along on a conveyor. The Four Star Candy Company on Mulberry Street was the place where I learned the art of wrapping lollipops. That was a short-term, part-time job. Other jobs included babysitting, combing and braiding hair, reading to older people (no charge), helping ladies in the kitchen, etc., and going on various errands. Of course, these jobs were all in our neighborhood.

I graduated from Charlton Street School in January of 1949, and I remember very vividly that my graduation dress was purchased from Fit Rite Fashions on Springfield Avenue.

Would you believe that after all these years, they are still in business? The next two years were spent at South Side High School (now Shabazz High School). Our family then moved to Bank Street, and Central High School was the school for that area.

After graduation in January 1953, the next September, I began as a freshman at Newark State Teachers College (on Broadway) in Newark, now Kean University, located in Union, New Jersey. After working for two years, I transferred to Winston-Salem Teachers College in Winston-Salem, North Carolina, now Winston-Salem University. I might add that I was the first in my family to go to college, and all praise and glory to God for favor and the journey. Back in the 1950s, I began using as my motto, "What I am is God's gift to me; what I become is my gift to God."

As a new student, I was required to arrive a few days before the other students. That was a very lonely time, not knowing anyone and coming from out of state. Language was strange. I remember one evening when I knocked on a door in my dorm, Pegram Hall (the junior/senior dorm). I was inquiring about pastries, and the response seemed like I had asked for something out of this world. Later on, I found out that they thought that I was "uppity" (that I was putting on airs of superiority). When the girls got to know me better, we all laughed.

After a few changes in roommates, Lizzie Brown, a beautifully saved young lady, became my roommate for the remaining years at Winston-Salem. Most of the students were going home for Thanksgiving, and Lizzie invited me to spend the Thanksgiving holidays with her family. Their home was in Lexington, North Carolina, and for the first time, this city girl saw how a chicken was killed. For a while, I could not eat chicken. Lizzie's family was very warm and hospitable to me.

Juniors were not allowed to attend church alone, so Lizzie and I usually went to church together. There were times when I went to church with Dr. and Mrs. Joseph Paterson. They had no children and took me "under their wings." I did not pledge to a sorority, even though Mrs. Paterson would have paid for me to join the Zetas. During my senior year, the Zeta Phi Beta Sorority selected me as their choice for Finer Womanhood Week. To God be the glory.

I was very active in the Student National Education Association (SNEA). I was also active in the Charm Club and the YWCA. One evening, I was privileged to travel with other students from the college; our destination was Women's College in Greensboro, North Carolina. What an experience! Truly, it was a once-in-a-lifetime event. The auditorium was filled to capacity, with standing room only! The famous American poet for the evening was none other than the renowned Robert Frost.

That evening, Robert Frost, with composure, stood there, center stage. His silver-white hair seemed to shine with brilliance. His voice was commanding as he shared his poetry with us. We applauded as he gave excerpts from his vast collection. One of my favorite poems is "Stopping by Woods on a Snowy Evening." That was also a favorite of many who attended, and as he concluded his presentation, all stood to applaud this great man, this American laureate. What an evening! That experience will forever be engraved in my mind.

Join me in reading the last four lines of "Stopping by Woods on a Snowy Evening":

> *The woods are lovely, dark, and deep,*
> *But I have promises to keep,*
> *And miles to go before I sleep.*
> *And miles to go before I sleep.*

The poem suggests movement, traveling on because there is so much to do, with the suggestion of commitments and promises to fulfill. We too have places to go and dreams to fulfill during our lifetime.

May this poem inspire you as it has inspired me to "keep on keeping on."

Normal college life continued. During my senior year, I received the Student Teaching Award for the spring semester, and the Ministers' Wives Alliance chose me as the one who best represented Christian character on the campus. My proud parents traveled from Newark, New Jersey, by train to celebrate with me, as I received the Bachelor of Science degree in Education. Since that time, I have received the Master of Arts degree in Special Education and the Bachelor, the Master and Doctorate degrees in Theology, and I give all the glory to God!

> *2 Timothy 2:15 reminds us, "Be diligent to present yourself approved to God, a worker who does not need to be ashamed, rightly dividing the word of truth."*

> *To this day, I still use the same motto I used as a college student: "What I am is God's gift to me; what I become is my gift to God!"*

The scripture that seems to gladden my heart the most is Psalm 139:14,

"I will praise You, for I am fearfully and wonderfully made; marvelous are Your works, And that my soul knows very well."

As I reflect on verse 14, I pause and consider the magnitude of God's great gift to you and to me. We are the crowning of God's creation—God's masterpiece!

Again and again, I will praise Him, for I am fearfully and wonderfully made.:

1. I am fearfully and wonderfully made physically.
2. I am fearfully and wonderfully made psychologically.
3. I am fearfully and wonderfully made emotionally.
4. I am fearfully and wonderfully made spiritually.

After graduation, I returned to Newark, New Jersey, and I felt the call of God on my life to the preaching ministry. I was somewhat hesitant in telling my pastor, the Reverend

Eustace L. Blake. Reverend Blake, on several occasions, had told me that I would make a good lawyer. When I shared what I perceived to be God's call, he answered, "Come on in. The water is fine!" He then said, "You will preach your 'trial sermon' next Wednesday at prayer meeting."

Several years earlier, I had taken classes on "love, courtship, and marriage" at St. James African Methodist Episcopal Church in Newark, New Jersey, and Rev. Eustace L. Blake was my instructor. He was also a friend and a great mentor. Reverend Blake was a man of honor and integrity, and he became my "father in ministry."

Long before I met Ohanio, Reverend Blake was praying for me to meet that special young Christian man. One day, Reverend Blake wanted to know from me, if I had also been praying. I told him, "No!" Then I went on to explain that if I asked God to send someone into my life, God would answer my prayer, but it might be God's permissive will and not necessarily God's perfect will.

My first teaching assignment was at Eighteenth Avenue School, also in Newark, then Cleveland Elementary School, and while I was actively working on my master's degree in special education at Newark State Teachers College in Union, New Jersey, I answered an ad placed by the Rutherford Board of Education for a teacher. Dr. David Brittain, the newly appointed superintendent of schools, interviewed me. He asked me to give him my philosophy of education, and I did, to the best of my ability. "You are hired. The job is yours!" I was hired as a third-grade teacher for Washington School. To my knowledge, I was the first black teacher that was hired. When I applied for the position, I had no idea that I would be hired.

Timing is everything. There was an opening for a special education teacher at Union School, and because I had already accumulated enough credits, I was selected and was transferred to Union School two years later. That appointment was right on time. The principal at Washington School was Mrs. Williams, and on August 10, 1963, I also became Mrs. Williams. Washington School only had one class per grade, and it was time to move.

After seven years of teaching special education, I taught fifth grade, second grade, and finally became the reading teacher at seventh and eighth grade levels for approximately thirty years. To this day, I still have many friends and solid relationships with the staff, parents, students, and community workers in and from Rutherford, New Jersey. Teaching in Rutherford was one of the best decisions that I have made.

The Inevitable

Ohanio and I met on June 22, 1962. I had no idea that he had Vera Johnson to point me out to him at the graduation ceremony held on June 3 at Manhattan Bible Institute in New York City. Ohanio had been trying to meet me for a whole year. When he heard the name Mary White called, he saw me and was content to go ahead with his vacation plans.

Ohanio told me much later that he had shared the following information with Vera Johnson, "If she is meant for me, I will have the opportunity to meet her upon my return from St. Croix," his birthplace.

About two weeks later, there was a revival at his church, Bethel Gospel Tabernacle in Jamaica, New York. Ohanio had attended the revival on Thursday evening and did not plan to return for the closing service on Friday evening. Reverend Frederick Hughes, a friend, invited me to the Friday evening service, and I agreed to attend the service. Reverend Hughes called Ohanio late that Thursday evening and told him, "I am going to your church tomorrow evening, and 'she' is going to be there!" Ohanio readily decided that he would attend the service again.

Reverend Hughes, the driver, along with other friends, Donald Carpenter, Effie Whittle, and Henry Soles, came to my home on South Sixteenth Street in Newark, New Jersey. We proceeded on our adventure. The passengers in the car had previously met Ohanio Alexander Williams because he was a friend of the late Apostle Arturo Skinner. When we arrived at the meeting place, Ohanio got in the car, quoting a scripture. His first words for all to hear were, "The Bible says that you should not add or take away from the Word of God. Psalm 16:11 says, 'In Your presence is fullness of joy; At Your right hand, are pleasures for evermore.' She is at my left hand." Was that a bold statement or not? He was quite cheerful. Evidently, I was not a disappointment.

The service was dynamic that evening. Afterward, we stopped for something to eat at the famous restaurant called Juniors, where they specialize in cheesecake, his favorite dessert. Ohanio announced to our group, "Order whatever you want." He paid the check for our entire group. He asked if he could see me again. I said, "Yes." Plans were made for him to have dinner at my home on the following Friday evening.

Friday came, and I prepared a colorful and delicious meal. Dinner went well; Ohanio complimented me on being an excellent cook. That very night, he asked my parents if he could marry me. No answer was given. My mom liked him immediately. My dad was not convinced. Ohanio was full of humor. He told a joke about a man who came calling on a young lady in the South. He went on to say that it was near the family's bedtime, and the young man had made no attempt to leave. The father asked, "And what's on your mind, young man?" The young man, stuttering, said, "I came to ask you for your daughter's hand in marriage." The father replied, "And what's wrong with the rest of her?" My mom loved Ohanio's humor. The evening ended with Ohanio asking me to go to Coney Island in New York on the following day. I consented.

We traveled on the PATH train. All the way over, Ohanio asked many questions. He asked if he could tell his mother about me. My reply was, "You don't have anything to tell her." The next question was, "Where would you like to live?" These questions and this "fast sweep" were too much for me to even consider. After all, I had made up my mind that I was not going to marry anyone for the next two years because I wanted to complete my master of arts degree in special education at Newark State Teachers College, now Kean University, located in Union, New Jersey. Having just met Ohanio, I was not desperate to get married, and he knew it.

Ohanio made it very clear that he was interested in getting to know me better. He lived in New York City on 137th Street and did not drive at that time. He traveled by train and bus to visit me at least once or twice a week. I liked Ohanio, and compared to some of the other young Christian men that I had met, we had more in common. Even though I liked him, getting married was not on my mind.

One evening, after making the long trip to my home, Ohanio said that he loved me but was not willing to come over as often if I was not serious about him. His direct manner was somewhat overwhelming for me. I told him that I had not planned to marry anyone for the next two years. I also said, "I am working on my master's degree, and marriage would interfere."

Ohanio made it clear that he was not interested in anyone else, and if I married him, he would see to it that I would finish my degree program. My friend, Effie Whittle, was not convinced that I needed to wait for two years. Her words were, "Mary, he really loves you!" She assured me that quite a few young ladies had their eyes on him. She reminded me that Ohanio was a Christian gentleman; he was handsome, well dressed, and he was also her pastor's best friend. Effie urged me to reconsider my thoughts about Ohanio and about marriage. She also said, "What about waiting for one year? In a year, you can get to know him." Effie was so certain that I was not going to meet anyone more suitable for me than Ohanio Alexander Williams, and she was right.

After my conversation with Effie, I did take some time to pray about what the Lord wanted for my life. I also gave myself a good "mental hygiene talk." I had been the first in my family to go to college, and at this point in my life, I was a teacher. Perhaps it was time to consider marriage, and I was twenty-seven years old. During that time, most of my friends stayed in the home of their parents until they got married, and I was able to assist my parents financially by staying at home.

My mom had some special qualities, which I will call gifts and graces. She was also a "dreamer." If my mom dreamed a certain thing, it became a reality. My mom was also a good judge of character, and Ohanio definitely had her vote. She said, "I feel like I have known him all my life." My father, however, had other thoughts. Because Ohanio was born in the West Indies, my father was very suspicious of him. He knew some men who were from the islands. He told me that they were possessive and very jealous. Time and experience teach us not to stereotype anyone, for there are good and bad people in every culture.

My dad realized that Ohanio was not like any of the other men. He finally told him, "You can marry my daughter if she wants to marry you, and if you are not going to treat her right, leave her here. We have never had any trouble with her." Ohanio assured my dad that he would take good care of me.

By August of 1962, I knew that God had sent Ohanio into my life, in God's time. I said yes to his proposal of marriage, and plans were made for Ohanio to meet my pastor, Rev. Eustace L. Blake. When Reverend Blake met Ohanio for the first time, he liked him instantly; he felt that his prayers had been answered. After a few counseling sessions with both of us, Reverend Blake gave his blessings. Reverend Blake told me privately that if he had a daughter, he would not mind his daughter marrying somebody like Ohanio.

We made plans for the wedding to take place one year later, on August 10, 1963, with the understanding that Reverend Blake would officiate at the ceremony. By this time, I agreed that Ohanio could tell his parents about me, and that, he was proud to do so. Soon after our conversation, I was invited to his home to meet his parents. His stepmother, Miriam, prepared a very delicious meal, with a Caribbean-Cruzan flair. Both parents were happy for us.

During that summer, we spent quality time together, enjoying recreational activities, including picnics, amusement parks, and visits with family and friends. We juggled our schedules to attend services at St. James AME Church in Newark, New Jersey, and Bethel Gospel Tabernacle in Jamaica, New York. Ohanio's "spiritual brother," the late Apostle Arturo Skinner, had also been a part of Bethel. We affectionately called him Brother Skinner. Ohanio met with Brother Skinner and told him that he had met someone special and that he planned to get married.

Because Ohanio kept a bag packed for traveling, Brother Skinner had doubts about Ohanio getting married. Ohanio convinced him that he was getting married the next year and asked him to be his best man. Brother Skinner invited us to the Labor Day celebration held at the Deliverance Center in Newark, New Jersey. We attended the service, and near the end of the service, Brother Skinner asked us to stand. The auditorium was packed to capacity, and Brother Skinner made the following announcement, "My brother has told me that he is getting married next August, and I am to be his best man!" There was great excitement in the church. I am told that many of the young ladies were very upset, especially when they found out that I belonged to the Methodist Church. I knew what they were inferring (that my spiritual growth was less than theirs). When I was sharing with Mom Stewart, she remarked, "You have the goods. You have the baptism of the Holy Spirit! You qualify!" Stereotyping and putting people in a "box" is a dangerous thing.

Sometime later, Ohanio suggested that I look at engagement rings, and I went to his favorite store, Macy's Department Store at Thirty-Fourth Street in New York City. Of all the rings that I looked at, the Marquis "caught my eye." The jeweler put the ring aside. Ohanio also looked at rings later that evening, and the one he selected was the same one that I liked, the Marquis, and one Friday evening in October,

Ohanio came to my home with the ring. What an exciting evening it was! After he proudly placed the ring on my finger, I "flashed" my hand for all my family to see, and I still proudly wear it today, after all these years.

Making plans for a wedding on the tenth of August, teaching school, working on the master of arts degree, and serving on the ministerial staff at my home church proved to be a real challenge. God, however, was faithful and brought us through with great joy and victory. Not only were we excited about the wedding but our families and friends also shared this special time in our lives. Dinners, invitations, and special gatherings were planned just for us.

During this time, we also attended the wedding celebration held for Eileen and Richard Christie on the Saturday before Thanksgiving of 1962. That celebration was held at Manhattan Holy Tabernacle (NYC). Dr. Edward H. Boyce was the pastor and also president of Manhattan Bible Institute. Eileen and Richard were on the staff and members of the church. Ohanio introduced me to some of his friends who also attended the wedding, and nine months later, the Christies attended our wedding at St. James AME Church. We enjoyed the Christies' company and spent times of fellowship together before and after our wedding.

The first surprise shower that was given for me was a "white shower," held on Saturday, January 12, 1963; it was hosted by Mary Mickens, a dear friend of our family and a member of St. James. Our annual revival was conducted by the late Reverend Dr. Mary Watson Stewart of Detroit, Michigan, and Mary Mickens wanted "Mom Stewart," my "mom in ministry," to be a part of that experience. Mom Stewart had already met the groom-to-be and liked him very much.

Mary Mickens served a delicious meal. Then the gifts were presented. Every gift was exquisite and personal. I can still remember the lovely white-laced peignoir set with satin ribbons, designed especially for a bride on her honeymoon.

Effie Whittle, my "maid of honor," gave me another surprise personal shower at the Jones Street Hall in Newark a few weeks before the wedding. The gifts from both showers supplemented and complemented my attire for the honeymoon and beyond. Who wouldn't feel special, lovely, and excited as I looked forward to a new phase in my life!

During this era, I might add, bridal gifts were personal gifts to the bride, not like wedding gifts that are given today.

Mary Jackson, a member of St. James and a close friend to my mom and me, made our beautiful and delicious wedding cake. She was an excellent cook and wanted to do something very special for me, and she did. We were able to freeze the top part of the cake and serve it for our first anniversary. Mary Jackson furnished everything for the "bridal table" at the unbelievable cost of sixty dollars. What about that! That is what love will do!

Ohanio could always tell me and others how many more days until our wedding day. On one of those Friday evenings, when Ohanio was at my home, my dad just happened to look out the window, and it was snowing. He asked Ohanio, "Did you look outside?" When Ohanio looked outside, he remarked, "One day, I will not have to go back home!"

We continued to make plans for the wedding. Seven bridesmaids and seven groomsmen made up the wedding party, with a flower girl and a ring bearer. We planned a "rainbow wedding" with beautiful pastel colors. My wedding gown was an exquisite designer gown from the Vera Plumb Shop on Bellevue Avenue in Upper Montclair, New Jersey.

During this enchanting time, this unbelievable time, the day before the wedding, I parked my car in front of the bridal shop. In my excitement, I forgot to put money in the meter. The meter maid had already begun to write the ticket. She was very apologetic; I think that it was a five-dollar ticket. That was the "bittersweet" of that day, and nothing could really spoil this special time. The rehearsal and the dinner were to take place later that evening, and the next day, I was to marry the man of my dreams, Rev. Ohanio Alexander Williams.

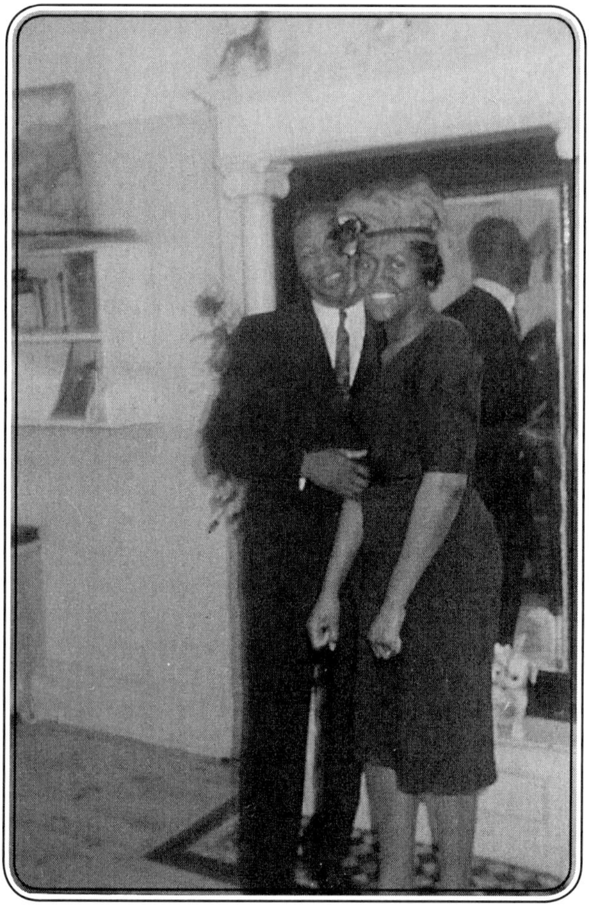

A Time of Preparation

During counseling sessions, information concerning marriage expectations should be provided. The couple should be ready and open to ask questions and talk about their strengths and weaknesses. These sessions can provide the couple with a realistic approach to marriage. Expectations that are unrealistic and self-serving can be discussed and hopefully modified to the satisfaction of both partners.

The opportunity for Christian growth is available through premarital counseling, and couples are encouraged to develop their spiritual lives. This will enable them to build a stronger marriage. Beginning the marriage with a Christian emphasis pleases God.

Amos 3:3 asks, "Can two walk together, unless they are agreed?" Joshua 24:15 sets the standard for the Christian home, "But as for me and my house, we will serve the LORD."

A warning for anyone who is considering marriage: Please do not date someone who is not saved. You might say, "We are not serious. We are just good friends." If there is some attraction or some chemistry, go the other way. There is an old adage that states, "When you play with fire, you just might get burned." There might be that "unguarded moment" with your friend. Ask yourself the question, "Why am I dating this person?" If the answer does not line up with the Bible, end the relationship.

Preparing for marriage does not begin when you meet that "special person." Our formative years, our background, our culture, our experiences, for the most part, will determine the success or failure of the marriage.

We are all part of a family, and family relationships are the strongest influence in personality development. No people or nation can rise higher than the family, and yet there is a definite breakdown of the family unit, as most of us remember it. I can remember that our family sat down and ate together. During those times, we had the opportunity to share the events of the day. If we had experienced something that was great or something traumatic, our parents would decide how to follow up on a particular action.

We also had the extended family unit, which consisted of those who were also looking out for us, and we behaved in a certain way. Parents are entrusted with the responsibility to first be accountable to God, and then to their family. When children are asked who their role model is, it would be great if one of those answers would be "my parents"!

We cannot go back and undo the past, but we can begin where we are and strengthen the family. As a result, each person in the family will be better prepared for marriage when the time comes. When an individual feels accepted in the family, it helps that person to feel accepted by others. The family is the key in helping us to discover who we are and to feel good about ourselves. When we don't feel valued or respected, there is brokenness that we carry into marriage or any relationship.

A healthy Christian family is a great beginning for a couple contemplating marriage. Sound teaching that is cushioned with love is an excellent form of "preventive medicine" for crises in families or relationships in general. The family that is not afraid to show love toward each other assists individuals who will one day start their own family. The person, who has been taught to have respect for the body as the "temple" of the Holy Spirit, will have fewer guilt feelings in later years.

If you have learned to accept yourself and have accepted Christ as Savior and Lord, you will make a better and happier marriage partner. The Word of God has not changed and is still relevant today. Hebrews 13:4 declares, "Marriage is honorable in all, and the bed undefiled."

The person who is happy and "whole" in Christ will be a caring and unselfish person in love, courtship, and marriage. People who have an intimate relationship with God will not bring a multiplicity of weaknesses and inadequacies to the marriage but will bring healing and happiness; on the other hand, poorly adjusted people will bring failure to the marriage union. With prayer and proper guidance, some of these failures can be avoided.

The Christian family is modeled after the relationship that Christ has with the church. When a husband and wife love each other and give life and sustenance to their offspring, God is well pleased. The family that is happy and serving the Lord is a great witness in the community. The strength of any nation begins in the home.

Because there is so much sexual freedom in our society today, the family and the church must come together in prayer. The old adage is true, "The family that prays together stays together." Parents will have success when they stand together in prayer, teach family values, and read God's "love letter"—the Bible. Then and only then will they know what God requires from all who claim to be Christian followers.

Joshua boldly says in Joshua 24:15: "And if it seem evil unto you to serve the LORD, choose for yourselves this day whom you will serve; But as for me and my house, we will serve the LORD."

Whether an individual is interested in marriage or just being in a good relationship with friends, he or she must have standards. Christians, of course, are called upon to take the lead in living a godly life. Marriage, whether in America or other parts of the world, is in trouble. One reason for this present situation is due to lack of care and commitment in establishing the marriage union. So many couples come to the time when they would like to get married but have so much "baggage."

We were not born Christians; most of us have regrets. Even if our parents were Christians, each one must come singularly and make peace with the Lord. Once we have accepted Jesus as our Lord and Savior and turned from all that is against God's word, we are accepted into the family of God. The past is forgiven, and all our sins are cast into the "sea" of God's forgetfulness. God expects us to forgive ourselves as we have been forgiven by God. Now as Christians, we are to remember that our bodies are temples of the Holy Spirit, and the best gift that we can bring to the marriage partnership is a healthy body.

The Christian community can still "step up to the plate" and do the right thing concerning marriage and relationships. Those who are followers of Christ should at least be sincere in relationships. No one should get married because of physical attraction alone because physical attraction is not enough to have a marriage that will last for a lifetime.

Couples seem to take time to plan for that blissful day of the wedding, but how much time is expended for the marriage itself? Taking time out to plan and prepare for the marriage will extend the honeymoon for a lifetime.

Premarital counseling is very important for the following reasons:

1. Misinformation can be corrected concerning the marriage relationship.
2. Either one or both partners may have unreal ideas as to their role in the marriage contract.
3. Preconceived ideas concerning finances, sex, family ties, occupations, children, etc., along with several counseling sessions may be required to correct erroneous or unrealistic ideas.
4. Why are you getting married? This should be a fundamental question. Every couple should answer this question honestly. Are you getting married because you are tired of being by yourself? Are you getting

married because all your friends are married or getting married? Are you getting married because you feel awkward when you go out alone? Are you getting married because you feel that everybody should try it at least once? Are you getting married because you don't want to grow old, alone?
5. What do we have in common? How do we complement each other? This should be a main consideration.
6. This is the time to "come clean" and discuss anything that might surface later on after the wedding day. First and foremost, the couple should love each other, be great friends, and have mutual interests.

Consider the following: Is he or she a believer in Christ and does he or she attend church on a regular basis? When you discuss finances, ask your partner what his or her views are concerning budgeting, tithing, and giving in general.

During this time, list some of the activities that you can share together other than physical attraction:

1. What do you like about your partner?
2. Have you allowed time to learn about your partner?
3. What are your partner's likes and dislikes?

   Remember, you are planning for a lifetime. Keep in mind that you are imperfect and so is your partner.

Working together, with an understanding heart and an open mind for growth every day, will bring both of you closer to God's idea for a happy and fulfilling union.

What are you willing to give for the success of the marriage?

Is marriage "fifty-fifty"? Your answer to this question and other questions will determine whether or not you are ready for the marriage challenge. When Ohanio and I were discussing marriage with Reverend Blake, one of the questions was, "Do you think marriage is 'fifty-fifty?'" We both were in agreement and said, "Marriage is not 'fifty-fifty' but 100%–100% from each one! After answering several questions, Reverend Blake seemed pleased with our responses. He really was convinced that our marriage was ordained by God. Reverend Blake told me privately, "If I had a daughter, I wouldn't mind my daughter marrying someone like Ohanio."

Reverend Blake counseled us to never go to bed at night angry or not speaking to each other. I can honestly say, looking back through the years, we followed his advice.

The late Bishop Roderick Caesar, Ohanio's pastor and mentor, had already planted a wealth of knowledge concerning a successful marriage in Ohanio's head and heart. What a blessing that was for both of us. Bishop Caesar met with us and gave us his blessings.

Our readiness for a successful marriage appeared to be on target. We enjoyed many of the same things. My friends became his friends and vice versa. We went to church services, revivals, picnics, and many other events. All of our friends felt that we were right for each other, and we were.

Both of us believed in the sacredness of marriage and that marriage was in the mind of God when He created Adam and Eve. To us, marriage was a solemn and holy vow, as I knew Reverend Blake would say to us at the ceremony, "Not entering into it unadvisedly but reverently." After I committed myself and agreed to marry Ohanio, he remarked, "I don't have any children on the outside, and I don't believe in divorce." In a lighthearted manner, he said, "No matter what you do, I'm not leaving home." As we continued to talk, Ohanio said, "I have noticed that people in the church are getting married and divorced. You'll get a divorce over my dead body. There is going to be one Mrs. Williams I plan to get married one time, and no two women will be carrying my name.

That was strong language. Someone else hearing that conversation might have been offended. What it said to me was that Ohanio was serious about marriage and commitment. That "charged" and bold outburst let me know that I had indeed met the partner that God had intended for me. Ohanio was committed to God first, the marriage next, and then to me. He was a person of great humor and integrity.

The days ahead were exciting. After the date was set for the wedding, Ohanio began "the countdown." Would you believe that Ohanio began counting the days until our wedding day, August 10, 1963?

Both of us were saved and in Christian ministry when we met. Ohanio was an ordained elder in the United Pentecostal Council of the Assemblies of God, and I had just received my first ordination as an itinerant deacon in the African

Methodist Episcopal Church in Trenton, New Jersey. Because Ohanio was unselfish and kind, he told me that he did not expect me to leave my church. His words were, "We will work it out," and we did.

All of us must be careful of personal information about ourselves. If, however, you have already made up your mind that you have met your life partner, you must share those personal and private things with your future spouse. This will become a trust issue and a trust moment. Before you share your past, make sure that you have really sought God's wisdom concerning the matter. Timing is everything. God has already forgiven you if you have asked for forgiveness, but not disclosing information that could possibly affect your marriage is deceptive and wrong. If your partner truly loves you, what you share will be kept between the two of you. Then and only then can you have a God-honoring life together.

You might say something like this: "If I had to do it all over again, I would have made better choices for myself."

- If you decide that my past is too much for you to handle, I will accept that, even if it means that we will not be together.
- Do not give me an answer now; pray about what I have shared in confidence and get back to me.
- No matter what you decide, I want us to always be friends.

Finally, if you really, really know how to pray, I do believe with all my heart that God will work everything out for your best interest. God is omniscient. God knows whether the person you are considering as your partner for life is the one for you. God will always keep your secrets. Can your partner keep your secrets? Can you be trusted if the "tables were turned"? Confidentiality is big on God's list! Can you be a true friend? Matthew 7:12 tells us to do unto others as we would have them do unto us.

When someone shares personal and privileged information with you, what will you do with that trust? Can you be trusted even if the person did not say, "Don't tell anyone what I have told you"? Remember the old saying, "What goes around, comes around"! Proverbs 17:17 reminds us that "a friend loves at all times, and a brother is born for adversity."

Whether you are single or married, trust is necessary in every relationship. As you pray and build intimacy with God, you will be directed as to what to tell and what to keep private. James 1:5 reminds us to seek God for wisdom, for God gives generously without finding fault. God is concerned about everything that affects us. Philippians 4:6 is a constant reminder that God is always ready and willing to assist us, and all we need to do is "ask."

Let us read it together "Be anxious for nothing, but in everything by prayer and supplication, with thanksgiving, let your requests be made known to God."

Always remember, especially if you are married, that what happens in your house should stay in your house and what happens in your bedroom should not be the discussion at the hair salon or the barbershop.

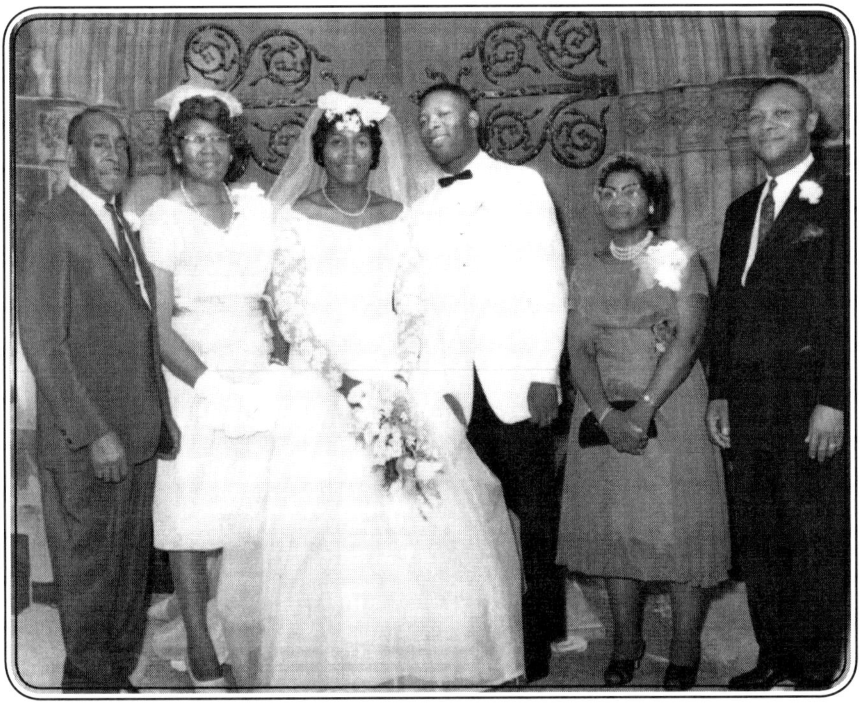

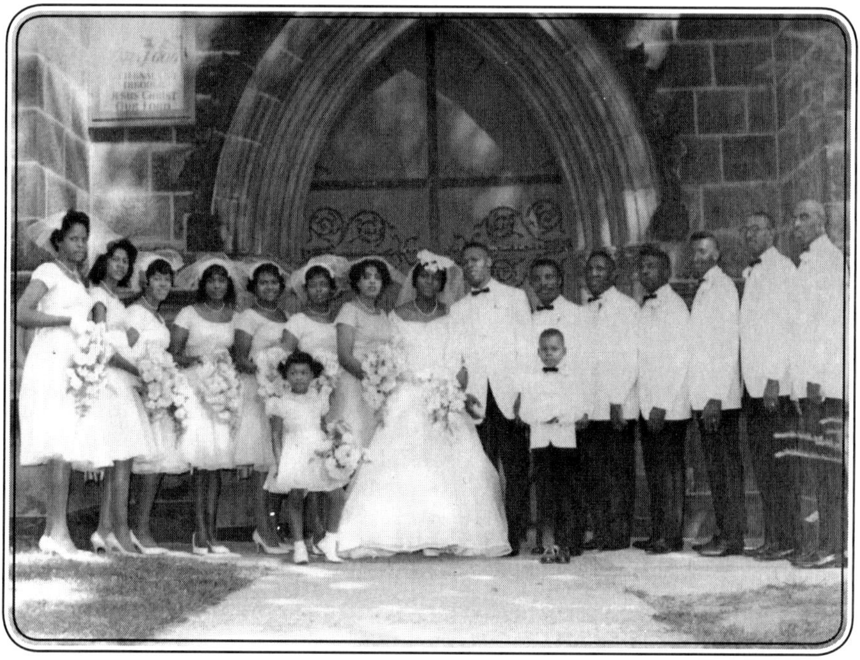

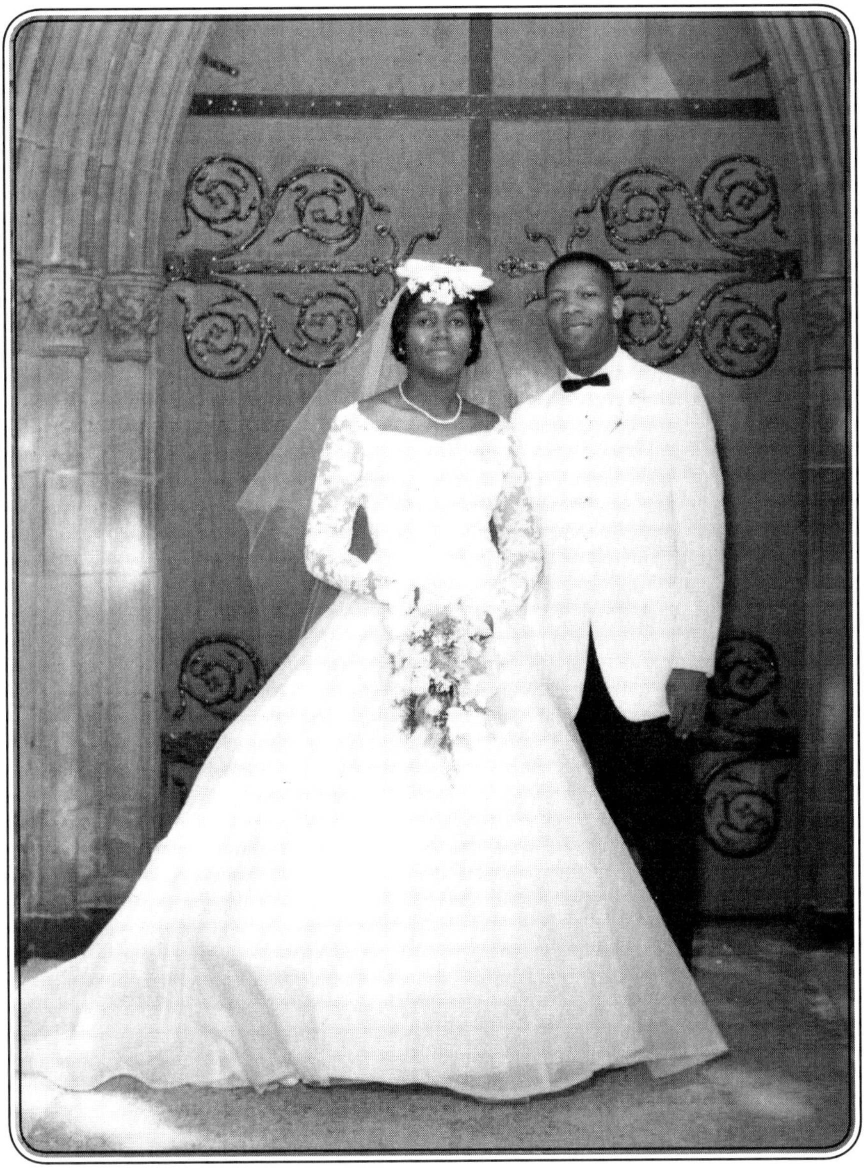

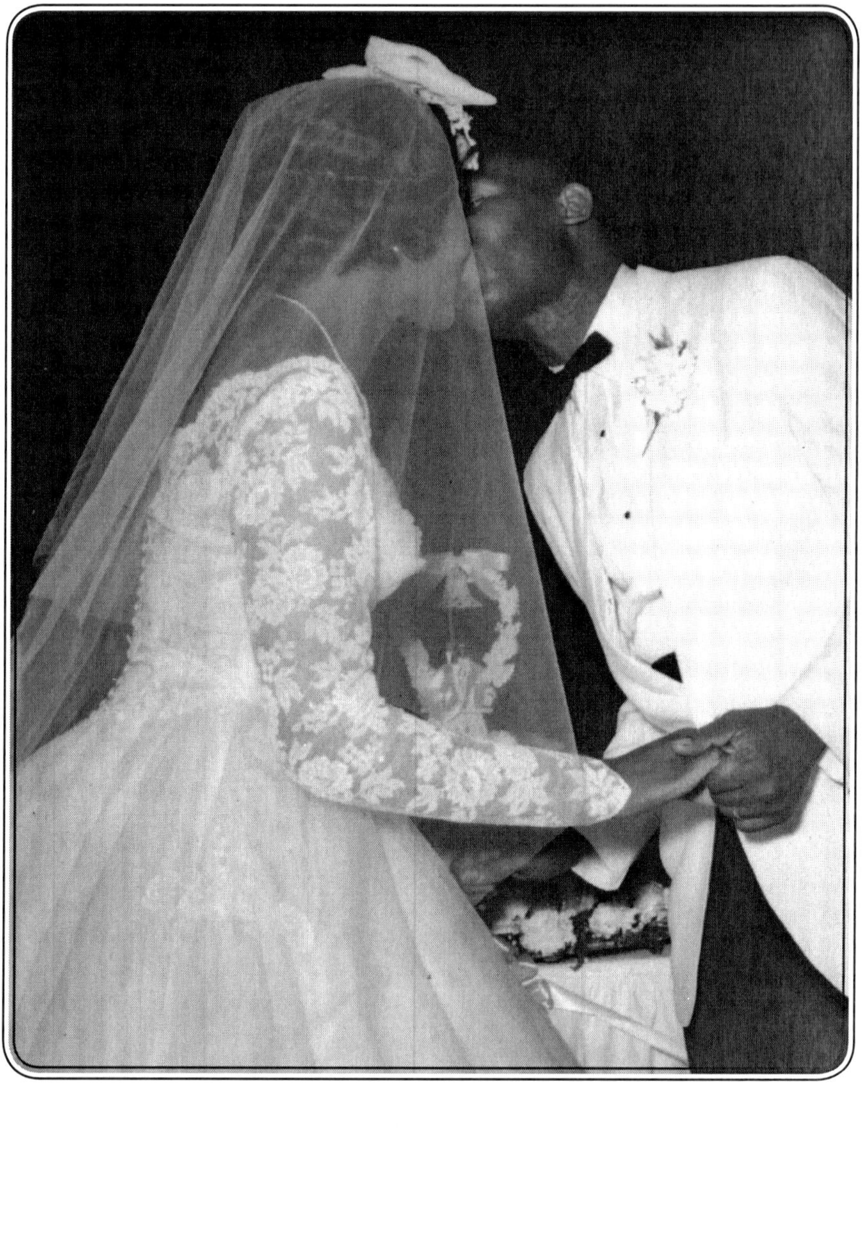

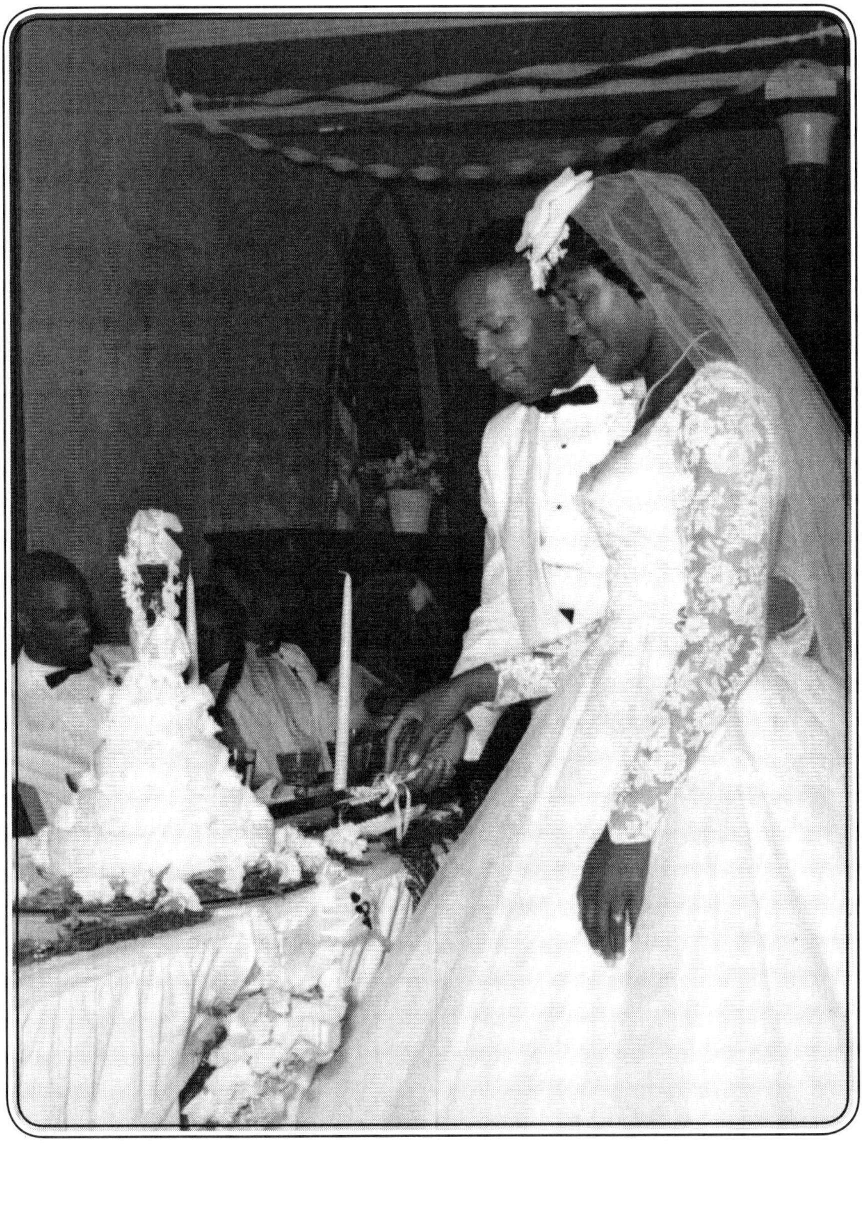

Wedding/Honeymoon

The "wedding announcement" had been placed in two local newspapers, *The AFRO* and *The Star-Ledger*. The photographer was Augusta Berns, located on the seventh floor in Bamberger's Department Store, downtown Newark.

Mrs. Bernice Coppock Johnson was our wedding coordinator. Bernice did everything possible to make our day special. She had a wealth of knowledge to share with us and was a faithful member and leader in our church. Bernice was a no-nonsense person but also had a great sense of humor. The rehearsal for the wedding was conducted with dignity, and the dinner that followed was great. There was laughter, fun, and fellowship on the evening before the wedding.

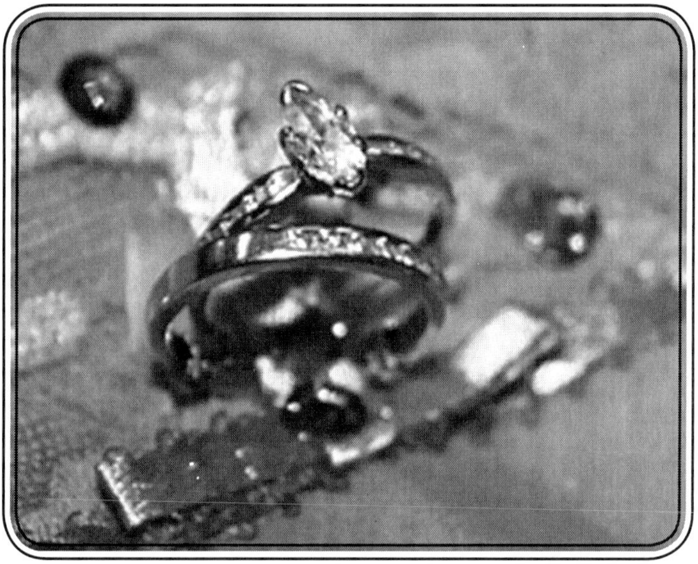

The Wedding

It has been said that no matter how well you plan, something always goes wrong, and on August 10, our "wedding day" was no different. Since Ohanio lived in New York, he decided to spend Friday night in our new apartment on Clinton Place. Ohanio had arranged that the attire for the groomsmen would be delivered to St. James AME Church; instead, the delivery was made at the Deliverance Church on Central Avenue, where his "best man" was the pastor.

Because Ohanio was "in place" and time was a factor, he called a taxi, picked up the suits, etc., and went to St. James, the place where they had agreed to dress. The day was saved! And the wedding proceeded on schedule at two o'clock in the afternoon.

St. James provided the perfect setting for our once-in-a-lifetime wedding. The architecture was superb with its ornate gothic arches that seemed to point heavenward. Completing this picture-frame setting was the stone walls of soft pale hues of pink and blue.

After the "bridal party," including the ring bearer and flower girl, had processed down the aisle and the "white runner" had been placed, I entered the sanctuary on the arm of my dad; it truly was a solemn moment as I walked down that long aisle, an aisle that I had walked down so many times before, but today, it was different. Today, I was going to begin a new life with the smiling groom who was waiting for me at the altar. The atmosphere was charged with warmth, love, and excitement. We exchanged vows and rings and pledged ourselves to each other as husband and wife, "until death do us part."

The "wedding reception" followed the wedding in the church's reception room upstairs. This was once called the Sunday School Room. The stage was beautifully decorated for the "bridal party." This was the same stage that I remember from earlier years, as many of the youth and adults performed in plays and various church activities. The entire room was lovely, and the bubbling fountain for the punch added to the elegance of the occasion. Colorful pictures of that wonderful moment in time are still being enjoyed today.

"Frozen in time" are the unforgettable memories of that special season in my life. I will be forever grateful to my parents, family, friends, and the participants of our wedding party.

After the reception, we went to our new apartment on Clinton Place in Newark, New Jersey. Mary Mickens, the family friend, who gave me the "white shower," had packed a special bag for us. She told us, "You are going to get hungry. Just wait and see." Mary Mickens was right. That evening, we were hungry. Her food was great. What a wonderful friend she was. She also packed the top of our wedding cake. We froze it because we were going to use it for our first anniversary.

No matter how well you plan, excitement can cause emotional and physical stress. Leading up to my special day, my monthly cycle started prematurely. I even went to my doctor to get something to help my situation, but nothing helped.

As we prepared for our first night together as Mr. and Mrs. Williams, surprise, surprise, surprise! It was the "moment of truth." I had to tell my new husband (in tears) that my monthly cycle had started. Ohanio was absolutely wonderful. He held me in his arms and comforted me. We were still hungry, so we raided the refrigerator. Then we slept and got up early the next morning, packed our car, and headed for our honeymoon spot in the Poconos. The scenery was breathtaking. We checked in and were just in time for our first meal.

Special events were planned during the days and evenings. We chose the activities that interested us, and by Wednesday, everything was back to normal for me. The title and the phrase "True Love Waits!" was a reality for us. Just a reminder for you and for me, sex is not the test of true love. Because Ohanio was a gentleman who was loving, gentle, and kind, we experienced intimacy and fulfillment as we consummated our marital union for the rest of our time in the Poconos. Most of us will agree that "practice makes better." Someone has said, "Don't worry about being perfect. You have the next twenty years to practice."

The Honeymoon

The "honeymoon" is described as the time after the wedding. Some consider the first month of marriage to be the sweetest and most harmonious time for the "newlyweds."

In 1 Thessalonians 3:12, it says, "And may the Lord make you to increase and abound in love to one another . . . " Ohanio and I were best friends and wanted the best for each other. Because he was so caring and attentive to me, I went out of my way to please him.

Since our wedding was on August 10, I had the rest of the month to make the adjustment to married life. For me, it was exciting to prepare meals for Ohanio, and he was not hard to please. When it was almost time for him to come home from work, I made sure that I looked special for him. After all, throughout the day, he saw other attractive ladies. From the time that I was a very young girl, I enjoyed looking my best. Just about the time for Ohanio to put the key in the lock, I made my way toward the door, and most of the time, I was there to greet him with a kiss and say, "Hello, honey!" Very often, he would say the same thing or say, "Hello, Mrs. Williams!"

We never fell out of love with each other. After Labor Day, I began teaching children with special needs at Union School in Rutherford, New Jersey. Everything was new, including my new name, Mrs. Williams. Ohanio was very supportive of all that I did. If he got home first, he would start the meal. Most of the time, I was the one who arrived home first.

During that first year, we spent quality time together. Because we both worked, we often did the laundry together, and as we folded sheets, towels, etc., we laughed, joked, and talked about anything and everything. We became great friends and wanted the best for each other. Ohanio and I dressed alike or blended colors that complemented what the other one was wearing even before we were married. Some referred to us as the "twins" or the "honeys"; to us, it was fun. During that time, I made some of the casual (African) shirts for Ohanio to blend or match what I was wearing.

As I mentioned earlier, Ohanio came from a humble background, and he always believed that God would allow him to have a better life than what he knew as a young boy. He had a grateful heart for the small things in life. Ohanio was never wasteful and was always looking for ways to bless the hungry and needy.

During the times that I traveled with Ohanio to the islands, family and friends alike would often refer to Ohanio's clothes. He looked good in whatever he wore. There were times that Ohanio would take a shirt or some other item and give it to the person, as he felt that the Lord was leading him. Ohanio was thankful that he no longer had to wear "hand-me-downs." Oftentimes, he would mail a particular item when he returned home. He seemed to have a joy in being able to give. I have heard him say on some occasions, "Their hands were longer than ours." Then he would explain that a family or a person was more financially able than his family. I often told Ohanio how great or how handsome he looked, and it was true. He was always well groomed no matter what he wore, whether going to church or going to work. There was no one that I knew who could take a simple stretch hat and shape it in a great style the way Ohanio did.

The summer after we were married, we did some "island-hopping," and Ohanio's boss asked him to collect an overdue debt from someone who lived in St. Thomas, US Virgin Islands, and it just happened to be one of our "stop-by places." While there, we were guests for lunch at Bluebeard's Castle. With Ohanio's charm and a letter from his boss identifying him, Ohanio was able to collect the past due debt.

God does move in mysterious ways. Even though I was involved in youth groups and other activities, I had never flown in an airplane. My first flight with Ohanio to his home was breathtaking. After we were airborne, I fell asleep, assured that I was in good hands, resting in the arms of the Lord. I was amazed at the mighty wonders of God as we soared to thirty-eight thousand feet in the air. What an awesome and majestic God we serve! What an experience it is to feel God's protection as I was cushioned in mounds and mounds of indescribable white clouds. There was no fear!

No artist can truly capture the wondrous works of our God. I join David in his assertion, "The heavens declare the glory of God, And the firmament shows His handwork" (Psalm 19:1).

After we landed at the airport, we went through customs and the usual procedures that involve traveling, especially when you leave the United States. We were excited to meet and greet family members during our stay in the Virgin Islands. Our trip also included a few days in Puerto Rico.

The hospitality was unsurpassed, and I had the opportunity to bond with family and friends. They all seemed to like me right away, and we stayed with his cousin, Mrs. Alma

Doward. Cousin Alma called me Niecey affectionately and made it a point to do so many extra things for me.

Her daughter and son-in-law, Eglantine and James Weeks, were also great hosts. All his relatives and friends treated me as part of the family. His cousin, Glenn, owned a bakery and supplied us with many goodies that just melted in your mouth. Special treats were prepared for us to take home. Because Ohanio was born on the island of St. Croix, the island will always be in my heart.

St. James had two services on Sundays, the 8:00 a.m. and the 11:00 a.m. services. Most of the time, we attended the early service; however, when the Young People's Choir of Bethel sang on second Sundays, we both attended and enjoyed the fellowship. Later on, Bishop Caesar assigned Ohanio to Bethel Gospel Church in Newark, New Jersey. Reverend Ohanio served faithfully as the pastor and worked with the founder, Mother Hattie Marshall. He felt led by the Lord to establish Ebenezer Gospel Tabernacle. As we did with Bethel Church, we started Bible classes under the leadership of Bethel Gospel Tabernacle.

The students had classes once or twice a week and were active participants in our Sunday evening worship services. We worked together as a team, and the Lord blessed our efforts. The yearly graduations were held at Bethel Gospel Tabernacle, and many of the students are still serving the Lord today in various ministries.

The Reaffirmation of Vows

The wedding coordinators for that special day were Mrs. Noami Huntley, Mrs. Bernice Johnson, and Mrs. Phyllis Snead.

Wedding Attendants

Mrs. Jenettha King	Mr. Wendol King
Mrs. Joan Francis	Mr. Lilbert Francis
Mrs. Virginia Minault	Mr. Edories Johnson
Mrs. Dolly Johnson	Mr. Timothy Brome
Mrs. Margaret Davis	Mr. Dennis Brown
Mrs. Effie Soles	Mr. Garvey Ince

It was time for celebration! After twenty-five years, we were more than ready to make this time, this occasion unique. How could we do that? We set the date as close to our original day as possible; that date was Saturday, August 13, 1988. We then contacted Rev. Dr. William D. Watley and secured that date. Our dear friend, Bishop Vernon R. Byrd, consented to give the "homily." Family and friends filled the church, and we reaffirmed our love and devotion to each other.

The church was packed with family and friends; the day was sunny and beautiful but extremely hot. We had the use of a white Rolls-Royce for the day. Usually, something goes wrong on such occasions, and on that day, the air-conditioning in the Rolls-Royce was not functioning properly. Nothing, however, could spoil our day.

Ohanio sang to me as we came down the aisle. The song went like this: "I love You, I love You, I love You, Lord, today because You care for me in such a special way. So I'll praise You, and I'll lift You up and magnify Your name. That's why my heart is filled with praise." The song was composed by William F. Hubbard.

Leaving, Cleaving, and Becoming One Flesh

Our model for marriage is established in Genesis, chapter 2:23–25, and it describes the first marriage union. Verse 24 gives an account of the three elements or essentials for marriage. They are, "Leaving, Cleaving, and Becoming One Flesh."

Without "leaving" one's old way of life, leaving the parent's home, and leaving space for what the new life holds or offers, the marriage cannot and will not survive. In reality, without "leaving," there is no marriage. In most cultures, a wedding ceremony takes place, and family and friends celebrate this new adventure with the couple.

Genesis 2:24 is clear in saying, "Therefore shall a man leave his father and mother." When a couple moves in or stays in the parent's home, their marriage is already in trouble. Leaving shows strength and maturity and not abandonment. Later on in life, there may be an opportunity for the couple to give financial assistance or whatever is needed as their parents grow older.

Leaving the parent's home physically is not sufficient. Taking the clothes and all the other belongings, just before the wedding, is a great start in the right direction. Some parents may have difficulty in "letting go" if a son or daughter supported them. If parents have been raising their children to become independent, knowing that someday, the children will become mature enough to start their own family, the whole process of "leaving" will be easier for everyone. Leaving the home where you grew up, leaving the family and comfortable and familiar surroundings can be very traumatic, but it must be done.

There are ways to make leaving less stressful. In some wedding ceremonies, I have seen the couple take the time to thank their parents for all that they have invested in their lives. In these instances, prior to the wedding day, letters or songs of appreciation have been prepared as part of the program. The bride usually takes the lead, and the groom follows. This can be a very "touching" and emotional moment not only for the parents of the bride and groom but for all who are present. Such an act of kindness, love, and appreciation can make the whole process of leaving less painful. The leaving process must take place so that the couple may begin their new life.

Living with either parent is not recommended. If the young man is not financially able to support a family, the wedding should be postponed. Borrowing money from family members or friends is a "taboo." Do not start your marriage by borrowing. If the finances are not in place, it means that you are not ready for this great challenge. God promises to give us the desires of our heart if we obey His commands. Try tithing, if your life is not going in the right direction. Remember always to do "first things first."

Malachi 3:10 says, "Bring all the tithes into the storehouse, That there may be food in My house, And try Me now in this, says the LORD of hosts, If I will not open for you the windows of heaven and pour out for you such a blessing that there will not be room enough to receive it."

God desires to bless us. Luke 6:38 says, "Give, and it will be given to you: good measure, pressed down, shaken together, and running over, will be put into your bosom. For with the same measure that you use, it will be measured back to you."

Genesis 2:24 says, "Therefore a man shall leave his father and mother and be joined to his wife."

Before one can "cleave," one must leave, and when God's design is followed, the couple are allowing themselves to become intertwined, fused, and they cannot be separated without being painfully hurt. "Cleaving" allows the husband and wife to become closer than anyone else on this earth. Intimacy will follow when "leaving" and "cleaving" take place. Some couples make the mistake of letting their children take the place of their partner. This is evident when the children consume all the time, especially with mothers who give little time to their husbands after the children are born.

Dating and spending quality time with your spouse are always in style. Dating between a husband and wife keeps the relationship fresh and special. The couple may not have the resources to be extravagant as before, but there are places and events that cost very little or nothing. I remember great times that Ohanio and I spent walking in the park and holding hands. What about sharing ice cream or some beverage together? We have all heard it said that "the best things in life are free." I have learned to live with expectancy and, every now and then, to "come out of the box," to do something spontaneous and enjoyable.

Cleaving to one's partner is easier when love is present. Marriage for any reason other than love is wrong. Marrying someone and believing that you can make that other person love you are an illusion or a fantasy. I have said it before, marriage without love is a nightmare!

Love is defined as a strong or passionate affection for a person of the opposite sex. (Of course, we are speaking of love according to the Bible.) To make room for that special person, your partner for life, you must put things in their proper perspective.

1 John 4:8 says, "He who does not love does not know God, for God is love." This God kind of love makes it easy to love a lifelong partner, when God is first in everything. This God kind of love, this "agape" love will stand the test of time. When a couple love God with all their heart, soul, and strength, "cleaving" will not be a problem.

When difficult days come (and they will), this divine love will hold, and the couple will find strength and "staying power." Divorce will not be an option. "True love" will be discussed more fully in the chapter entitled "What Is Love?"

Becoming "one flesh" is only possible when the other two prerequisites are in place—"leaving" and "cleaving." Marriage will then give two people, the husband and wife, permission and freedom to become "one flesh." The couple is no longer two but one in God's eyes.

There are many people who are embarrassed to talk about sex. Since God speaks about this union in the first book of the Bible, we should "come out of the box" and discuss sex openly in the proper setting.

Becoming "one flesh" in marriage has God's approval, and the marriage will be fulfilling and exciting for the "newlyweds." God's design is that sex and intimacy will follow after the wedding ceremony! Each partner will be looking forward to the wedding night with excitement, anticipation and not with guilt or regrets.

True love will wait. One partner might try to put pressure on the other concerning sex, especially when they have become engaged and the ring has been given. The man might say, "It's only a piece of paper" (referring to the "marriage license"). The license gives permission for a couple to be intimate and become "one flesh." Some may argue that sex is the test for love. Sex is not the test of "love."

Sex by two unmarried people is called fornication. See Deuteronomy 22:13–21. Christians should not be involved in fornication. If the man is honorable and he loves his bride-to-be, he will wait and not pressure her to have sex with him. The only sure way of not becoming pregnant or possibly having a sexually transmitted disease passed on to you is to wait. In many places, the blood test is no longer required. Our bodies are temples of the Holy Spirit. Having a blood test before marriage is the right thing to do. If you have nothing to hide, why wouldn't you want to have a blood test? I have heard it said, "All that glitters is not gold!" Having a blood test might save your life. If your partner suggests that you go out of state to get married (where a blood test is not required), I would have "second thoughts" about their faithfulness to you or their love and concern for you.

Becoming "one flesh" is not possible outside the bond of marriage. Living together without God's approval leaves the couple open to satanic attack and not the blessings of God. There will certainly be guilt, and in many instances, jealousy will follow. Children who might be born through this relationship deserve the protection, the rights, and the privileges of a Christian family. Marriage, in and of itself, is a challenge, and any intimate, sexual relationship outside of marriage is an insult to God.

True love will wait. Even after marriage, one partner may become hospitalized or go through some traumatic experience. If sex is not possible, will you stop loving the person? Love does not stop. Remember, sex is not the test of love. When we were newlyweds, one of Ohanio's relatives jokingly said, "Remember that married people still have 'cold nights'!" We laughed. If your partner loves and values you, he or she will put passion on "hold" and wait with love and expectancy. True love is worth the wait.

Becoming One Flesh

In order to have the full impact of "becoming one flesh," let us look at Genesis 2:24, and it states, "Therefore a man shall leave his father and mother and be joined to his wife, and they shall become one flesh." Becoming "one flesh" means more than sexual intercourse. Sex, however, is essential in marriage.

Because of sexual immorality, Paul wrote to the church. I might add that sexual immorality was in the church in Paul's day, and it is very much alive today. In 2 Timothy 2:15, we are reminded, "Be diligent to present yourself approved to God, a worker who does not need to be ashamed, rightly dividing the word of truth."

This word of truth is rightly divided by Paul in 1 Corinthians 7:1–5. Paul says, "It is good for a man not to touch a woman. Nevertheless, because of sexual immorality, let each man have his own wife, and let each woman have her own husband. Let the husband render to his wife the affection due her, and likewise also the wife to her husband. The wife does not have authority over her own body, but the husband does. And likewise the husband does not have authority over his own body, but the wife does. Do not deprive one another except with consent for a time that you may give yourself to fasting and prayer; and come together again so that Satan does not tempt you because of your lack of self-control."

Hebrews 13:4 is the best testimony or witness to the marriage covenant, "Marriage is honorable among all, and the bed undefiled; but fornicators and adulterers God will judge." From this passage, it would appear that sexual conduct outside of marriage is wrong or unacceptable to God. Leaving, cleaving, and becoming one flesh allows the couple time to bond together, grow together, thus becoming one.

Spending time together allows the "newlyweds" time to become observant of what motivates their partner. What are the "mood swings"? In spending quality time with your spouse, you learn what to say and what not to say.

In another chapter, I spoke about complimenting Ohanio on the way he looked. He was handsome, whether he was dressed for a special occasion or casually dressed. His response was a "thank-you" or a great smile.

When passing by your partner, in the privacy of your home, a gentle or endearing touch is always in order. When you take the time to study your partner, God, through the Holy Spirit, will reveal to you when and what is appropriate! I have found that it works like a charm.

Becoming "one flesh" may be difficult for some couples if they allow "the world" to dictate what God intended for them. Wives may look at marriage as control, especially when the word "obey" is used in the ceremony. The word "obey" was not intended for the husband to control his wife by saying, "The Bible says, 'you're supposed to do what I tell you to do.'" That statement is a "turnoff" to any confident and intelligent woman. If the husband truly loves his wife as his own body, the wife will be able to feel his care, love, and protection. The word "obey" in the wedding ceremony, if it is a problem, should be discussed during premarital counseling.

I don't remember Ohanio using the term "obey" to me in all our years together, and I have learned that you get what you give. When you live to love your spouse, and your spouse does the same, you have to win, and there will be "love and joy in the camp"! Too often, Christians take their "cues" from the "world" instead of the Bible. When we do not obey God's Word, we will "fall into the ditch."

The whole concept of "leaving, cleaving, and becoming one flesh," though a challenge, is possible when God is at the center. There is nothing too hard for God!

Back in 1945, Paul Westmoreland wrote a simple narrative ballad called "Detour." The ballad depicts the foolishness and waste of time by those who do not follow sound advice. These are words that have caught my attention: "Detour, there's a muddy road ahead. Detour, paid no mind to what it said. Detour, oh, these bitter things I find; should have read that detour sign."

The Lord has given us so many warnings and sound advice through the Bible, and it would benefit us greatly if we obeyed God's commands. Job 28:28 advises, "Behold the fear of the Lord, that is wisdom, And to depart from evil is understanding."

When you spend time in prayer and read the Bible on a regular basis, discernment will surely follow. Isaiah 30:21 assures, "Your ears shall hear a word behind you, saying, This is the way; walk in it, whenever you turn to the right hand or when you turn to the left."

Today can be a new day and a new beginning for us, if we repent and let go of the past. Lamentations 3:22–23 says,

"Through the LORD's mercies we are not consumed, Because His compassions fail not. They are new every morning; Great is Your faithfulness."

What Is Marriage?

First of all, marriage was God's idea! God initiated marriage as a covenant and as an institution. God intended marriage to be a lifelong commitment. The whole account is recorded in the first book of the Bible, there in the garden of Eden. Genesis 2:18, 21–25. Verse 18 says, "And the LORD God said, It is not good that man should be alone; I will make him a helper comparable to him." Verse 21 says, "And the LORD God caused a deep sleep to fall on Adam, and he slept; and He took one of his ribs, and closed up the flesh in its place; Then the rib which the LORD God had taken from man He made into a woman, and brought her to the man. And Adam said: 'This is now bone of my bones And flesh of my flesh; She shall be called Woman, Because she was taken out of Man.' Therefore a man leave his father and his mother, and be joined to his wife, and they shall become one flesh. And they were both naked, the man and his wife, and were not ashamed."

This union, this coming together was God's plan to fulfill and cause the first perfect marriage, the ultimate union between a man and a woman. The marriage was to be a spiritual covenant in a perfect environment. Marriage, then, gives two people the permission to become "one flesh." No one else but God could have thought of this "holy institution," this blissful union but God! Hebrews 13:4 is very clear, "Marriage is honorable among all, and the bed undefiled." The hope for marriage to last for a lifetime must be ordered by the Lord.

Many get married today for the wrong reasons. When people are lonely or have been hurt, they are very vulnerable to someone showing them attention or kindness. The attention is new and exciting. Some women want to become mothers, and they are anxious about their "biological clock," motherhood. Some are desperate, and they choose wrong. Philippians 4:6 reminds us not to be anxious about anything but to make our requests known to God in everything, by prayer and petition with thanksgiving. There is nothing wrong with wanting to get married; make sure, however, that your pursuit toward this end is of God.

It has been said that "the eyes are the windows of the soul." If your whole agenda is on getting married, the "could be" person that you meet will sense your desperation, and that is a definite "turnoff"!

When I met Ohanio, I was not looking for a husband. Proverbs 18:22 says, "He who finds a wife find a good thing. And obtains favor from the LORD."

What are you willing to sacrifice to have a happy and fulfilling marriage? I ask the question because some couples are not very honest with themselves or their partners. There are some couples who have gotten married and still spend so much time with "buddies" or their "sister friends." They have waited, in many instances, for years, and now that they have been blessed with a "mate," they are still going out with their single friends on a regular basis, and many of them go on vacation with friends, etc., and not their spouse. There is something wrong with that picture. Could it be that some people have not "counted up the cost" of what marriage is? Could it be that they are in love with the "title" or the "idea" of marriage?

When two people decide to get married, they must be willing to break all ties that would jeopardize their marriage. This is especially true if the friend is of the opposite sex. Yes, we can still have friends. If we pray earnestly about our relationships, God will help us. I have another question for you, If you are not willing to change anything from the past, why do you want to get married? Marriage is a sacrifice, and each partner must be willing to deny himself or herself in order to bring out the best in their partner.

If families have done their best in loving and caring for their children, the "dividends" will be great, for their children will not be starved for attention and affection and looking for love in all the wrong places.

When looking for the right partner, it is of utmost importance that you be the right person. I was a committed Christian and very involved in church activities long before I met Ohanio. I was nurtured by caring and loving parents, the St. James family, and other Christian groups. I was not perfect, and no one is, and I could not imagine marrying anyone who was not a believer in God and faithful in doing God's work.

To have a lifelong, happy, and fulfilling marriage, it is crucial that both parties have the same goals. I knew that I was not going to get married just to prove that I could or to see how marriage works. Marriage for me was to be a lifelong commitment and contract.

God has planned that marriage should be the ultimate of all human relationships and last for a lifetime. When we stand before God, the minister, and all who come to witness our wedding, we should be totally convinced that the marriage has been ordained by God. The vow, "until death do us part," should be genuine. Our mind was made up that only death would part us. Marriage is not for the "weakhearted"; marriage is hard work and a challenge. Nevertheless, it is worth the challenge. In a marriage, there are two imperfect people with specific needs. With the love of God, love for your new life partner, and sensitivity, the needs of each one will be met. If, however, either of the partners is deficient in any area, the other partner suffers. Marriage was never intended to fix broken people. Marriages can, in many instances, help those who are already dysfunctional when they are sincere and ask for guidance. Jeremiah 32:27 speaks to us today and forever, "Behold, I am the LORD, the God of all flesh. Is there anything too hard for Me?"

When we face up to it, many of the problems or difficulties that couples face did not begin in the bonds of marriage; they began long before they met. Somewhere within the personality structure of at least one of the marriage partners, there was some brokenness. That is why premarital counseling is so vital. When couples have asked me to perform their ceremony, I make it very clear that they must participate in premarital sessions with me.

During these sessions, weaknesses, erroneous ideas, and other issues can be discussed openly. Some ministers advise on having a couple meet separately and then meet together.

Personally, I recommend that the couple meet together for each session. In my experience, what is shared between the minister and one of the partners is really "one-sided." For a marriage that is designed to last for a lifetime, honesty, integrity, and openness must be "out in the open." Any question and any concern should be confronted before either one approaches that special day, the wedding day.

Family differences and family relationships must be considered along with discussions of love, sex, money, children, etc. With the right attitude and with God's help, marriage can be very successful and rewarding. Marriage is 100 %–100 %. If I live to please my husband and he likewise lives to please me, we will be happy, and we were for thirty-three years, until God called him home.

I cannot remember a time when Ohanio got up from the dinner table and did not tell me, "Honey, I enjoyed my meal." I made it a point to praise Ohanio for unexpected and kind acts. There were so many times that he brought me special gifts, and he would, from time to time, stop at his favorite store (Macy's) and bring me a treat, and I made it a habit to do special things for him. Most of the African shirts that Ohanio wore, I made them to match my outfits. It was my delight. The life that we shared complemented both of us, and there was a feeling of mutual respect.

Ohanio had a way of looking at me when I was leaving the house, either with him or without him or on special occasions. He would say, "Let me look at you. I don't want anybody laughing at you." That was his caring way of making sure that everything was properly in place. I heard Ohanio make this remark more than once, "You're the best thing that ever happened to me. God has already arranged it. I'm going first. Just in case I'm wrong and you go first, I am going to sell the house and go back to St. Croix."

When we give this partnership, this lifelong relationship our all, 100%–100%, we will both win, and we have won. In the game "tug-of-war," there is one rope and two teams. Each side, each team wants to win. The strategy for winning is that each team member must pull with his or her total energy and strength to win. In marriage, the same strategy is essential for total fulfillment.

How appreciative I was when Ohanio would start the meal if he came home first. Whatever he prepared was always acceptable and appreciated by me. He made it plain to me that he did not want a tired wife. Ohanio was always thoughtful, caring, and helpful. He did not leave his clothes all over the house, and he further stated, "If I wanted a maid, I would have hired one." Who wouldn't like that kind of attitude and that kind of partner? Love and kindness beget love and kindness! Because of who he was and his great love and care for me, I did not mind preparing special meals for him, especially buttermilk biscuits once a week. My biscuits were special to him.

In looking back and realizing the blessings of the Lord, I find it easy to be grateful to God and will forever praise Him. Psalm 103:1 says, "Bless the LORD, O my soul; And all that is within me, bless His holy name!"

Marriage Is a Learning Experience

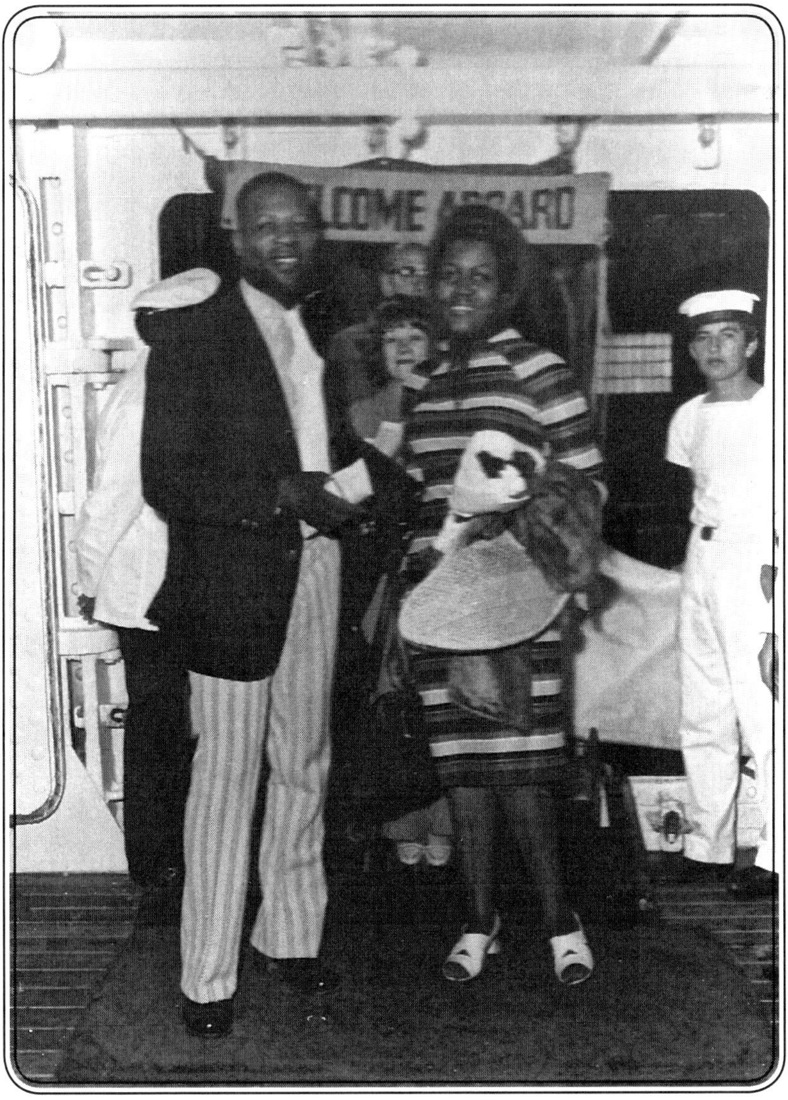

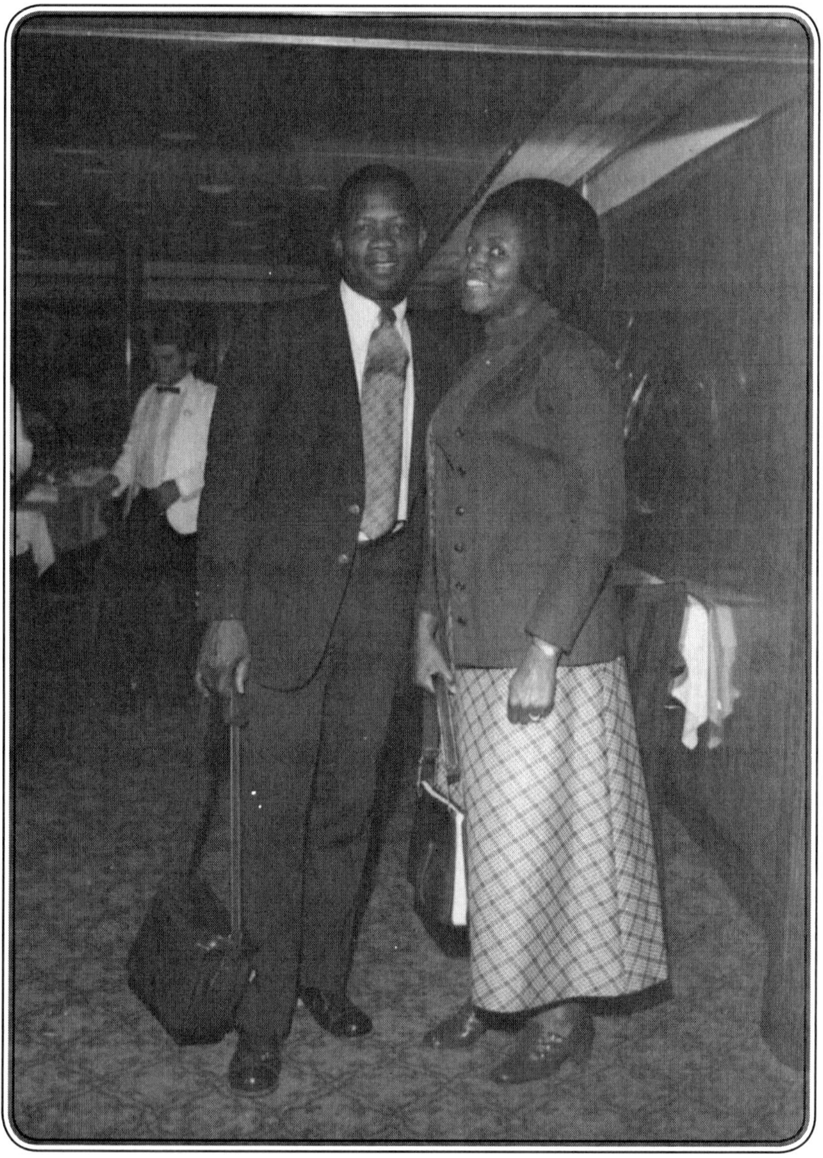

There is no book or manual that has all the answers or can guarantee you that your marriage will be a happy and fulfilling one. One thing that I have learned in my walk with the Lord is that God is faithful and is concerned about everything that concerns me. As I continue to trust the Lord and follow the Lord's leading, I will be successful in all my endeavors and especially in my marriage. First of all, I am to give the Lord first place in my life. Matthew 6:33 says, "But seek first the kingdom of God, and His righteousness, and all these things shall be added to you." God wants me to be happy and fulfilled. After all, God did ordain marriage. 3 John 2 declares, "Beloved, I pray that you may prosper in all things and be in health, just as your soul prospers."

I had gone on a few dates before I met Ohanio, but there was no one that I really considered to be my lifelong partner. I have discovered that when we really come into a relationship with God, the "blinders" come off, and we no longer see the world through "rose-colored glasses." Those trivial relationships before I met Ohanio would not take me to the places that God had planned for my life, and I was not in a hurry to get married.

I had already taught school a few years in Newark, New Jersey, and while working on my master's degree in special education and teaching in the Rutherford, New Jersey school system, I met Ohanio. The rest is history. Ohanio was the one chosen by God for me. I tried to learn as many things about Ohanio as I could. Even though he did not drive, he was always on time when visiting me. He took the PATH train from New York, the 25 bus and then walked two blocks. Later, he learned that it was better to take the 107 bus, and he did not seem to mind. Ohanio was a gentleman and well groomed all the time. Everything matched. He also had a great sense of humor. He was not arrogant, and most people were comfortable in his presence.

He shared with me concerning his humble beginning in St. Croix. I enjoyed talking with him and hearing his terrific accent. "Island food" has always been intriguing and delicious to me. Ohanio came from a background of good cooks, and he enjoyed good home-cooked meals. That put me high on his list (smile). He was also a great cook.

Ohanio wanted me to meet his dad and his stepmother. I was invited to dinner, and they liked me, and I am glad that they did because Ohanio had already made up his mind that I was to be his lifelong partner. My dad was the one who was not sure or convinced that Ohanio was the right one for me. Because he had met some men from the Caribbean who were jealous and possessive, he prejudged Ohanio. We are wrong when we stereotype people without getting to know them. There is another saying, "Time will tell" (TWT). Ohanio proved to my dad and all who met him that he was a person of character and integrity.

Whether we were on vacation, visiting friends, shopping, or doing ministry, God allowed us the opportunity to witness the goodness of the Lord. We always had colorful tracts. Ohanio used his ministry cards, and I used the Mary White

Williams Ministries, Inc. cards and newsletters. Every day can be a rewarding "learning experience" in marriage. We had our differences because we were different; however; we were never disagreeable. Reverend Blake had reminded us years before, "Never go to bed not speaking to each other." When you really love God, pleasing God is the ultimate goal.

Proverbs 15:1 says, "A soft answer turns away wrath, but a harsh word stirs up anger." Saying the right words can save or restore a marriage or a relationship. Proverbs 25:11 declares, "A word fitly spoken is like apples of gold In settings of silver."

We are all imperfect people, and there are times when we jump to conclusions. God loves us and says to us in those times, "Be still and know that I am God." When we don't know what to do, do absolutely, positively nothing! I knew that our marriage was to be a witness to the faithfulness of God, and I loved God and wanted to be a good wife. Proverbs 12:4 says, "An excellent wife is the crown of her husband, But she who causes shame is like rottenness in his bones."

Even though we made mistakes, we were never rude to each other; at times, we were silent because we did not know what to say. Before we were married, Ohanio announced that we were not going to have twin beds or separate beds. I can honestly say that we never went to bed not speaking to each other.

On one occasion, we did not agree on the kind of garage door to get. Ohanio wanted a door that you could lock with a key, and I wanted a door that, by pushing a button, would be operable. Eventually, we had an automatic door installed. When we were returning home one evening, it began to rain very hard. Ohanio said, "Honey, you were right about the door. We don't have to get wet." He pushed the "door opener," and we drove right into the garage. We did not argue about the door, and we both won!

For several years, Ohanio worked at the Print Shop in New York City, and after taking the train from New York to New Jersey, then taking a bus from Penn Station in Newark, Ohanio welcomed a good home-cooked evening meal with me. Truly, it was my joy to know that he was so appreciative of the effort that had gone into *the meal, and I can still hear his words,* "Thank you, Honey. I enjoyed my meal!" There is an old saying, "The way to a man's heart is through his stomach." Proverbs 14:1 says, "The wise woman builds her house, But the foolish pulls it down with her hands."

We enjoyed doing things together. Ohanio helped me set the table when we had dinner guests. Whatever the decor, it was fine with him; he always wanted to know what he could do to help me. He enjoyed saying, "My wife," and he had no problem washing the dishes after a meal. Even though he is gone, I still use some of the ideas and special things that I learned from him.

Ohanio was unselfish; he visited hospitals, prisons, nursing homes and did not want to see anybody hungry. Whether it was Penn Station or Weequahic Park in Newark or Haiti, Ohanio took the time to share clothing and food. He never forgot his humble beginning.

During our marriage, we complemented each other in ministry by giving money and clothing whenever possible. Ohanio made several trips to Haiti, assisting Missionary Rosetta Lee and Rev. Dr. Annabelle Freeland in their individual missions. Bishop Frank Curtis Cummings says, "If you can't go, you can send go!" Although I did not travel with Ohanio and others to Haiti, I helped with goods and money. Ohanio was a pastor with missionary zeal.

Communication Is Key

Communication is key to a successful marriage. During my courses of love, courtship, and marriage, that was one of the main points that Reverend Blake stressed. He said that the lines of communication must always be open. One main point was, "Never go to bed angry and not speaking to each other."

As we were planning for our life together, Ohanio let me know early on that he did not believe in having twin beds. That thought was never in my mind. In fact, he said, "I'm not having twin beds in my house!" The wedding gift that Ohanio purchased for us was a very unique bedroom set, with a full-size bed and a triple dresser and chest, with two night tables. The set was and still is classic and in use today. Communication was not a problem. We never turned our backs to each other and refused to speak. This does not mean, however, that we were always in agreement on every matter. Reverend Blake told us that you could disagree without being disagreeable.

What we did when one of us was out of line, we would come back with a statement or scripture, something like, "You do plan to preach on Sunday!" or "You are going to church!" We were implying that you had to be a doer of the "Word," or you need to practice what you preach. We were both ordained ministers and using scripture verses helped us to stay focused and in tune to God and each other.

During our first year of marriage, I drove to a friend's house so she could use my typewriter. Typewriters were in use and in style back in the days before computers. I had already told Ohanio my plans. After visiting my friend, we shopped a little, and I stayed longer than I had intended. Even though I called, Ohanio was very upset. It was on a Saturday afternoon. Upon my return, Ohanio was not his usual charming self. His face was like "six o'clock"! That is how he referred to his actions. (He had a long face.) He had cooked dinner to surprise me. Well, I apologized and told him how sorry I was. He said to me, "I guess ladies don't shop like men." Ohanio realized that he had overreacted, and he did not want anything to upset our marriage. He also apologized for his behavior.

We enjoyed a wonderful meal together, and I said, "Thanks, honey, for the meal." That incident taught Ohanio how to give me some space, and we both had our close friends. The next day, Ohanio preached a wonderful sermon, sharing some of his experiences from the previous day. "To God be the glory!"

I am reminded of a couple who were not on very good terms. They lived in another state and were not speaking to each other. For identity purposes, let's call them Larry and Paula. Paula had stopped cooking for Larry on a regular basis, and when she did cook, she would let the dishes that he used pile up in the sink. When Larry asked her why she did not wash his plates, etc., she told him to wash his own plate. She further told him that she was going to start using paper plates. After an argument, Larry made the mistake of pushing Paula. She said that he hit her. Did I tell you that they were members of a church and that they both claimed to be Christians? After their struggle or episode, Larry went to church. After all, it was Sunday. Paula stayed home. When Larry came home, he found that his clothes were all placed in a pile on the living room floor. Things did not get any better. They refused counseling and are divorced.

What went wrong in their marriage? As I remember, they did not go for premarital counseling. Premarital counseling is a prerequisite for any couple hoping to have a successful marriage. I don't know what went wrong! When we are in a covenant with God and our future partner, such behavior will not happen. It has been said, "A house divided against itself cannot stand."

In another chapter, "Becoming One flesh," I mentioned that you should learn your partner's "mood swings." When couples spend quality time together, each one learns what to say and what not to say. Many years ago, Ohanio and I were in the car. I remember that he was the driver. He hit his finger. I sensed that he was in some discomfort. I asked him if he wanted me to drive. His answer was, "Don't be ridiculous!" Maybe I was too sensitive, but I felt hurt. After all, I was just trying to be caring and considerate. The word "ridiculous" was a real "trigger" for me. In my mind, I was thinking of the meaning of the word. At the moment, I became silent and unresponsive. As an educator, a teacher, I read more into the word than what was intended. He was not trying to hurt my feelings. He was not calling me ridiculous or silly. Ohanio was really saying, "It's no big deal. I am able to drive." He interpreted my reaction to the word "ridiculous" that he should never use that word around me because I did not like the word. That was not the reason. I just overreacted. Sometimes, it is not the word itself; it could be that we might be going through something at the time.

That was early into our marriage. Since then, I have learned to take myself less seriously and not to overreact. A close friend of ours told one of the members of the church to "drop dead!" The next Sunday morning, she greeted him, and he remarked, "Last Sunday, you told me to drop dead. Make up your mind," and they both laughed. Words are powerful. They can heal, or they can destroy. Proverbs 25:11 reminds us, "A word fitly spoken is like apples of gold in settings of silver." That old adage, "Think before you speak," still applies. Once the words are out of your mouth, you cannot take them back. James 3:5–6 reminds us to control the tongue: "Even so the tongue is a little member, and boasts of great things. See how great a forest a little fire kindles! And the tongue is a fire, a world of iniquity."

We must learn to make our words appropriate for the action. In marriage, as in other meaningful relationships, it is unwise to give ultimatums, such as, "If you do this, I will do that!" "If you leave now, don't bother to come back," etc. Solomon is considered to be the wisest man who ever lived. In the book of Ecclesiastes, he is called the Preacher. He taught the people by word and by example. We should be reminded to think before we speak. If we say harmful and damaging words, we cannot take them back. "The Preacher sought to find acceptable words; and what was written was upright—words of truth" (Ecclesiastes 12:10).

On one occasion, Ohanio and I were shopping at Bamberger's Department Store in Newark. Ohanio just happened to meet a friend while I was in another area of the store. Usually, we were seen together, and the friend asked, "Where is Mary?" Ohanio replied, "We split up!" When Ohanio noticed the shocked expression on the friend's face, he explained that I was in the store but at another location.

"Communication is key!" So often, I say, "I know you think you understood what you thought I said, but I am not sure that you realize that what you thought you heard is not what I meant!"

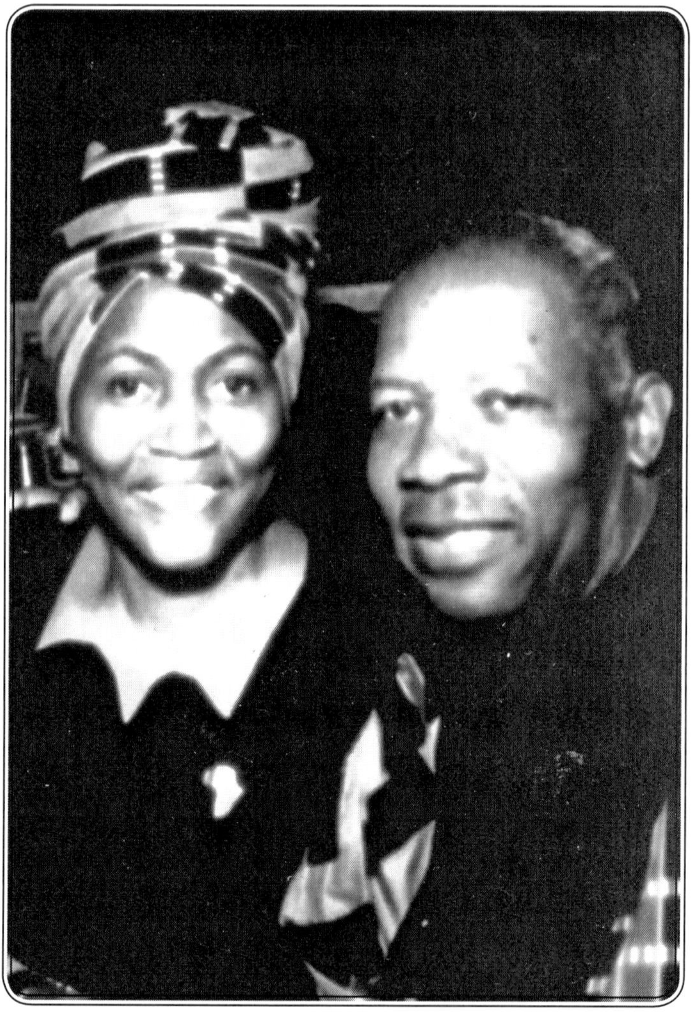

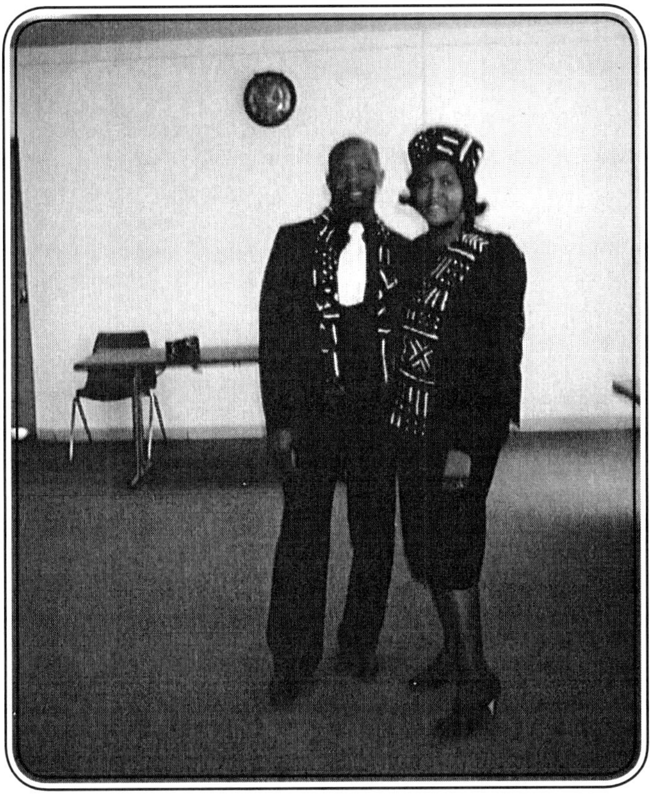

Some of Our Sayings and Scriptures

I have heard it said that "there is nothing new under the sun." Solomon, in the book of Ecclesiastes 1:9–10, affirms, "That which has been is what will be, That which is done is what will be done, And there is nothing new under the sun."

The following are some of our favorite sayings and scriptures:

Ohanio's Sayings and Scriptures

- I was a midnight rambler, seeking joy for my sin-sick soul.
- The Bible says that you should not add or take away from the Word of God.
- Psalm 16:11 says, "You will show me the path of life; In Your presence is fullness of joy; At Your right hand are pleasures for evermore."
- When we met for the first time, I was sitting on his left, and Ohanio said, "She is sitting on my left, and I will have pleasures forevermore."
- I'm not going to let anyone break up my marriage.
- You have to handle some people like a t-shirt—when it gets dirty, you throw it off.
- You have to handle some people like glass—fragile.
- She was wearing her pants so tight; it seemed like she was poured into it.
- If you go out there and get pregnant, remember, it takes nine months to get here and eighteen years to grow up.

- There's nothing wrong with wearing a fur coat as long as your husband's money paid for it.
- There is nothing wrong with driving a Rolls-Royce as long as you are not robbing God.
- I help Mary around the house the best way I can so that God will let me have her a little longer.
- A bull's horns are never too heavy for his head.
- Don't leave home as a johnnycake and come back a "dumpling."
- Because Ohanio knew that I tried to eat well and take care of myself, he would jokingly say to me, "You are going to live until they take you out and sun you!"
- Proverbs 17:17 says, "A friend loves at all times, And a brother is born for adversity."
- You don't have to be at every dog and cat show.
- I don't need a tired wife; if I wanted a maid, I would have hired one.
- You don't fight fire with fire—the fire department is still using water.
- Isaiah 3:10 declares, "Say to the righteous that it shall be well with them."
- Live while you can and die when you can't help it.
- There's a job out there with your name on it.
- When someone complained about the heat or said, "It's too hot!" Ohanio would often reply, "Hell is hotter!"
- People buy what they want and beg for what they need.
- Ohanio often said and taught that "a church is not a church unless it is a 'missionary church.'"
- Don't let the world rub off on you—you rub off on them.

Some of Mary's Favorite Sayings and Scriptures

- You tell some, and you keep some.
- Obey the next thing the Holy Spirit tells you to do.
- When you don't know what to do, do absolutely, positively nothing!
- Study to be quiet.
- Live with an attitude of expectancy and leave room for interruptions.
- Make plans and leave room for interruptions.
- You can't build happiness on someone else's unhappiness.
- What goes around comes around.
- Don't take any wooden nickels today.
- What I am is God's gift to me; what I become is my gift to God.
- Anything worth doing is worth doing right.
- Pray directly, specifically, and to the point.
- Try to see the glass "half full" instead of "half empty."
- "He has shown you, O man, what is good, And what does the LORD require of you but to do justly, To love mercy, And to walk humbly with your God?" (Micah 6:8)
- "I will praise You for I am fearfully and wonderfully made; Marvelous are Your works; And that my soul knows very well." (Psalm 139:14)
- Isaiah 50:4 says, "The Lord GOD has given me the tongue of the learned, that I should know how to speak a word in season to him who is weary: He awakens me morning by morning, He awakens my ear To hear as the learned."

- Your attitude determines your altitude.
- Show me your friends, and I'll tell you who you are.
- Others can; you may not!
- Two wrongs don't make a right!
- Don't throw in the towel.
- "And let us not grow weary while doing good, for in due season, we shall reap if we do not lose heart." (Galatians 6:9)
- Be yourself, before you'll be by yourself.
- "Oh that men would praise the LORD for His goodness, and for His wonderful works to the children of men!" (Psalm 107:8, 15, 21, 31)
- A place for everything and everything in its place.
- "There are no bargains on the counters of life; the way to succeed is to take the road that leads to success, and keep going until you get there."
- There is none so blind as one who will not see.
- Every tub has to sit on its own bottom.
- Practice makes better.
- Misery loves company.
- At this time in my life, I can pick, choose, and refuse.
- It is better to be safe than sorry.
- "I know you think you understand what you thought I said, but I am not sure that you realize that what you thought you heard is not what I meant."
- There is no time like the present.
- Don't put off until tomorrow what you can do today.
- Whatever!
- "I'll see you, if the Lord is willing and the creek doesn't rise."
- You don't have a nickel in that dime.

- It is better to be single, wishing you were married than to be married, wishing you were single.
- Wait for the second ring.
- If you can think it, you can have it!
- "Lord, what exciting things are we going to do today?"
- Speak up for the persons who can't speak for themselves.
- The way you start out is the way you will end.
- Dream, plan, and put into action!
- I saw it in my mind's eye.
- There's the reason that we tell people, and then there's the real reason.
- Shun the very appearance of evil (see Proverbs 3:7).
- Remember, a liar must have a good memory.
- It is better to have it and not need it than to need it and not have it!
- Say what you mean and mean what you say!
- Proverbs 15:1 says, "A soft answer turns away wrath, but a harsh word stirs up anger."

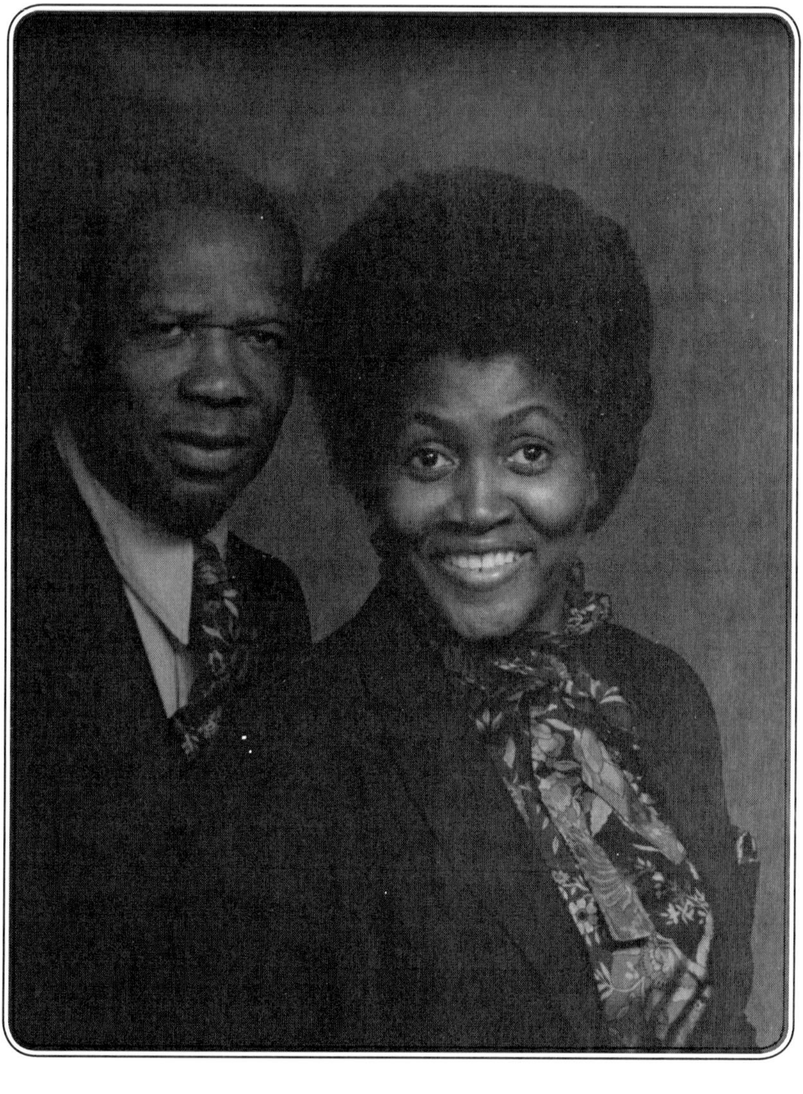

Complimenting Made Easy

Complementing One Another

The word "compliment" is a noun and refers to an expression of esteem, respect, affection, or admiration; it can be an admiring remark, honor to present with a token of esteem. A compliment is an expression of praise, congratulations, or encouragement. Proverbs 5:15 says, "Drink water from your own cistern, AND running water from your own well." To some, the grass is always greener on the other side of the fence. The answer to that is, "Mow your own lawn." Learn to say kind words to the "love of your life." Say words that will encourage and affirm. Proverbs 25:11 says, "A word fitly spoken is like apples of gold in settings of silver."

The following are compliments that you can use. You can change the words to fit your special person (these are just suggestions):

- Honey, the day that I met you was one of the best days of my life.
- You have a great sense of humor.
- You are handsome, or you are beautiful.
- I love your accent, or I love your voice.
- What a blessing you are to me.
- I am proud of you.
- You are so caring and thoughtful.
- I enjoy spending time with you.
- You smell good.

- I love the way you_____.
- That outfit looks great on you.
- Honey, I am glad that I married you.
- You always make me feel so special.
- You are the "love of my life."

Because Ohanio was such a wonderful helper to me while I was working to complete my doctoral work, I wanted to do something for him to show my gratitude. The following letter was engraved in gold, in a red setting and placed in a gold picture frame.

To My Beloved Husband

OHANIO ALEXANDER WILLIAMS

However, Through The Years, We Have
Affectionately Called Each Other, Honey.
Honey, This Day I Gladly Share With You
Because We Are One!
Thank You For All Of Your Love,
Encouragement, Friendship, And Sacrifices.
God Made You Very Special And
Gave You Especially To Me.
All My Love - All My Life
From The Doctor That You Helped To Make,
Your Wife,
Mary
June 27, 1982

The word "complement" is a noun and refers to something that makes whole or supplies what is lacking. Just to give you an example: Ohanio's presence could light up a room. He knew how to tell a joke and would get most people to laugh, and I am more serious but also enjoy a good laugh. Reverend Blake was happy that I had met someone like Ohanio, and he said that Ohanio brought that missing link, "the laughter" into my life.

We complemented each other by the way that we cared for each other. We enjoyed spending time together. There were times that I did not particularly care about certain television (TV) programs, but I also knew that Ohanio wanted me to watch the program with him, so I did. We did many things together. Not too long ago, I read a Christmas card that he had given me some years ago, and he always signed his cards, "Your true love, Ohanio."

We enjoyed dressing alike or coordinating our outfits, then going out together. Those were great times. Our friends often teased us and said, "You look like brother and sister." Ohanio would quickly respond, "But we know better!" Ours was not a jealous or controlling love. We gave each other space to grow and breathe.

Back in 1988, when I started the Mary White Williams Ministries, Inc., Ohanio encouraged me to use my name. He believed that God had given me the ministry, and whatever he could do, he seemed happy and proud to do it. There were times when Ohanio "ordered me" to go upstairs and rest and whatever I was supposed to do, he did it joyfully.

Some of those times, he would say, "I don't need a tired wife." Ohanio assisted me in so many ways—he helped with mailings, conferences, retreats and even as a chauffeur. For nine years, Ohanio served as the vice president, until his home going in 1997. These were some of the things that we did together.

Because Ohanio was a Christmas gift, we celebrated his birthday (for several years) with a formal table setting in the afternoon on December 25. With a very festive decor, Ohanio and I joyfully set the table together. After I had shown him what went on the table or how to place the napkins, etc., he would tell me, "You do something else, something I can't do." Those were happy and memorable times with family and friends. Even though Ohanio was born on December 25, I always gave him a birthday and a Christmas gift.

As the years passed, we stopped the formal celebrations and started celebrating the New Year with family and friends, sometime between Christmas and the New Year. What I remember most is that we planned and shared together. This also included washing the dishes, separating decorations, and putting things away for the next year.

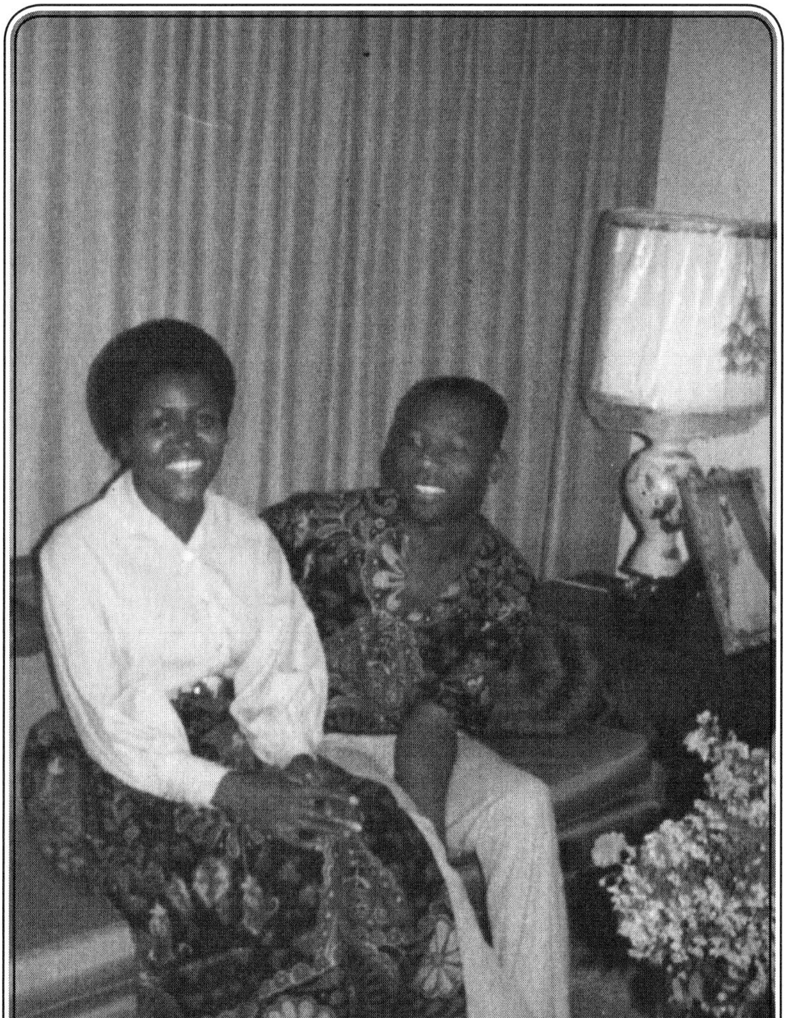

What about Children?

From the very beginning, the family was on God's mind. The account given in Genesis 1:27–28 says, "So God created man in His own image; in the image of God He created him; male and female He created them. Then God blessed them, and God said to them, 'Be fruitful and multiply, fill the earth and subdue it.'" The family is the foundation of any society and is still on God's heart and mind today.

During premarital counseling sessions, family planning, along with other issues that will affect the couple's life, should be discussed freely and with all honesty. This is not the time to keep secrets. "Honesty is always the best policy." There is a saying, "A liar must have a good memory."

Some couples enter marriage, hoping to change their partner's mind, and that is not what usually happens. If you just happen to remain silent when the counselor asks the question about children or you shrug your shoulders, you are not ready for marriage. One partner might answer, "Whatever my partner wants, that is what I want!" That is not a realistic or honest response. You or your partner may not even want children. If that is the case, just say so. Any answer that is not the truth is called deception. Now deception hinges on trickery and double-dealing. "Child of God," now is the time to "say what you mean and mean what you say!"

If parents are blessed to have children, they have a moral responsibility to present their children back to God. Hannah longed for a child (a male child). During the time in which she lived, it was almost a disgrace to be married and not have children. Hannah desperately sought God, and God gave her a son; his name was Samuel. She was so appreciative of God's great gift to her that she presented him back to God. You can read about this Bible account in 1 Samuel 1:1–28. Samuel lived in the temple, and once a year, Hannah visited him and made him a beautiful coat.

When our actions please God, we are rewarded by God. Elkanah and his wife, Hannah, received a fivefold blessing of three sons and two daughters. "How great is our God!" Because of God's great gift to them, you can be sure that their home was a place of love and worship. Yes, God is still in the "blessing business" when our lives please Him.

Children who are loved, trained, and cared for are more likely to grow up and model the home that they remember. Proverbs 22:6 says, "Train up a child in the way that he should go, And when he is old he will not depart from it." Parents, for the most part, determine the future of their children.

When children are surrounded by love and respect, they usually do well in every way. Differences in points of view should be openly expressed in the home without fear of mistreatment from any family member. When all parties are valued and respected, others will notice and use that family and home as a healthy model.

Godly parents will do well to protect the lives of their children in every way. Even though society has changed immensely, it is still the responsibility of parents to give guidance to their children, for children are often "shortsighted" and see in the present, in the now. If parents will be the role models that God demands, their offspring most likely will follow their pattern of life. Sometimes, children will become contrary or rebellious. Parents must always remember what their role is. For the most part, if godly examples and fair guidelines have been established, children will usually comply.

Ephesians 6:4 further states, "And you, fathers, do not provoke your children to wrath, but bring them up in the training and admonition of the Lord." The same as adults do, children respond to love, fairness, kindness, and understanding.

Having children can be a great blessing. If, however, you want to have children so that they can help you, your motive is wrong. If you and your spouse are desirous of having children and God blesses you to be parents, love and nurture them as unto the Lord. Remember also that they are only on "loan" to you from the Lord. Prepare them to love God, to be respectful to everyone, to be accountable for their actions, and to become independent.

During my many years of teaching, preaching, and doing evangelistic work for the Lord, I have tried to pour love, care, respect, and life skills into the lives of children and young people, as the opportunities presented themselves. Because of my ministry and involvement with them, I am included in their family gatherings, rites of passage and bridging ceremonies, graduations, showers, and so much more.

Often, I receive cards, notes, and letters, reminding me of words, scriptures, etc., that Ohanio and I have poured into them. The praise belongs to God for allowing us the opportunity to make a difference in the lives of people, especially children and young people. Galatians 6:9 says, "And let us not grow weary while doing good, for in due season we will reap if we do not lose heart."

Those who say that they have been "born again" have a responsibility, "a charge to keep"! As Christians, we are to be a witness in our home first and then a witness in the world.

Honesty between life partners is the only way that the two can "become one flesh." If you do not want children, say so. If the love between the couple is genuine, in time and with prayer, God could cause the attitude of one spouse to change. The main thing is to be honest with each other, even if it means that the marriage will not take place. As a Christian, that is the risk that you must take. Who knows, through honesty and time away from each other, there might be a change of heart and mind.

Philippians 4:6 says, "Be anxious for nothing, but in everything by prayer and supplication, with thanksgiving, let your requests be made known to God; and the peace of God, which surpasses all understanding, will guard your hearts and minds through Christ Jesus."

Down through the years, we have sung this familiar chorus, when we have gone through trials and hard times, "Take your burdens to the Lord and leave them there." When we give our burdens to the Lord, in prayer, the Lord will always give us the victory.

Get busy doing the work of the Lord, and you will be greatly blessed. During the time that I was preoccupied with thoughts of being a mother and especially having a little girl, I met a woman who was very spiritual and prophetic. She prayed for me and spoke into my life concerning the great things that God was ready to do in my life. Many doors have opened to me, and I am grateful. My travel has been extensive, and God continually raises up sons and daughters who love God and are a blessing to me. And I still believe: "What goes around, comes around!"

Words Have Power!

Words do not define who we are. Many times, words are spoken that can either heal or wound us, "beat us down" or elevate us. Proverbs 25:11 says, "A word fitly spoken is like apples of gold in pictures of silver."

On several occasions, when Ohanio and I had dinner guests, the question would somehow surface, "Do you have children? You have so much to offer!" We heard the term "childless." That term or expression was piercing to us, as if to say that we were less or incomplete. Even though we have no biological children, we have sons and daughters "everywhere." Some are godchildren; some have been born into the "kingdom of God" because of our ministry. As a couple, we have never felt less or incomplete but truly blessed. We adopted a more suitable term, "child-free."

During one season in our lives, we were in agreement concerning adoption. I really wanted to adopt a little girl. After some soul-searching and serious prayer, I came to the conclusion that I was the one pressing for the adoption. Ohanio wanted to please me, but it was not God's perfect will for us. God would have allowed it; it would have been God's permissive will but not God's perfect will. God has blessed our lives greatly, allowing us to help children and adults in the United States and abroad.

During our ministry, Ohanio and I have stood in the gap for many young people and adults, as we served in the role of pastor, mentor, and friend. Because we took time with them years ago, today, they still remember, and we are close. Sometimes, your own biological children are not available when an emergency arises. I can honestly say that if there is a need, all I have to do is make a call, and the Lord usually prompts the right person to take care of that particular need.

In numerous places, there are people who have been strengthened and encouraged by our ministry. Some of them, from time to time, have reminded us of something that we said, and that saying or scripture has become so meaningful in their daily lives. I give God all the praise for the opportunities that we have had to be godparents so many times and to be considered and respected as a family member. It's a "God thing"! How grateful we are for all the sons and daughters who have come to faith and are serving the Lord here and abroad. "To God be all the glory!"

The closeness of the relationship that we have shared has allowed each one of them to greet me as they desire. To some, I am Pastor Mary; to others, I am Pastor Williams. Still, others call me Mom or Dr. Mary. God is a god of variety, and I am rich because of the people who are in my life. There is a saying that "if you would have friends, you must first show yourself to be friendly."

The Myth of "Playing House"

Let us first define the word "myth." A myth is a noun that denotes a traditional or legendary story, usually concerning some being, hero, or event with or without a determinable basis of fact or natural explanation. A myth can be any invented story, idea, or concept. A myth can also be referred to as a tall tale or a fantasy.

Some years ago, a young lady came to me, all excited about her future marriage. To protect her identity, I am calling her Sherrie. This is what Sherrie shared with me, "Dr. Mary, the Lord told me that Reverend Thompson [not his real name] is going to be my husband." I know Reverend Thompson very well, and he had said nothing to me about getting married to Sherrie. Now this is what Sherrie did: She called Reverend Thompson's office, and she set up an appointment to speak to him concerning some urgent business. This is what she said to him, "God told me that you are going to be my husband," and the reverend replied, "Go back to God and tell Him that I don't want you!" Sherrie left his office in tears. She was heartbroken but also "silly." That was only a fantasy of Sherrie's mind, and it was only a myth.

Just in case you know someone like Sherrie, male or female, please advise them that even if they believe that they have a revelation straight from the throne room of God, they should exercise some wisdom. The wisdom is to keep that information to one's self until it becomes a reality. All of us need to pray for God's wisdom. James 1:5 tells us that if we lack wisdom, we are to ask of God, and God will give us liberally. Even though Ohanio proposed to me when he came to my house for the first time, there was no way that I would have said yes to such a proposal. I was not a desperate woman then, and I am not a desperate woman today.

I live and perform at another level as noted in Psalm 139:4, "I will praise You, for I am fearfully and wonderfully made; Marvelous are Your works; And that my soul knows very well." For all who are waiting for that special someone to come along, continue to trust God. Pray specifically, without giving God a timetable. Be happy and secure in your singleness. You are not incomplete. You are the "crowning of God's creation"; you are a masterpiece! Colossians 2:10 says that you are complete and whole. Whether you are single or married, you are complete and whole. When you are single, you are free to come and go as you please and free to spend your own money. In marriage, "me," "my," and "mine" are not appropriate, if you are seeking oneness.

God loves you and wants you to be happy. If you are destined to have a life partner, God will make it happen, even if the person is in another part of the world. May I remind you that Ohanio was not born in the continental United States but in St. Croix, US Virgin Islands; it was never in my mind to settle for less than God's best for me. At times, we hinder the plans of the Lord because we become restless and impatient, and when we become impatient, we settle for less than God's best. When we settle for less than what God intended for us, misery and regrets are sure to follow. For greater encouragement in this area, please read Jeremiah 29:11–14.

Timing is everything! God promised Abram that he was going to be a father. Sarai, Abraham's wife, became restless and impatient. Genesis 16:1–16 reports the entire account of Abraham's and Sarah's actions. The first four verses will give us a vivid picture of what happens when we try to hurry God.

Now Sarai, Abram's wife, had borne him no children. And she had an Egyptian maidservant whose name was Hagar. So Sarai said to Abram, "See, now the LORD has restrained me from bearing children. Please go into my maid. Perhaps I shall obtain children by her." And Abram heeded the voice of Sarai. Then Sarai, Abram's wife, took Hagar, her maid, the Egyptian, and gave her to her husband, Abram, to be his wife, after Abram had dwelt ten years in the land of Canaan. So he went into Hagar, and she conceived. And when she saw that she had conceived, her mistress became despised in her eyes.

Sarai's plan "backfired"! Instead of solving a problem, other problems arose. Hagar begins to look upon Sarai with contempt. In other words, Hagar began to show disrespect and treated Sarai as one who was worthless. Not only did Hagar show Sarai disrespect but she also despised her mistress. (See verse 4). Can you just imagine how this drama might have played? Sarai tells Hagar to prepare something for her, and Hagar replies, "Get it yourself. I am the real wife. I am going to have Abram's child. You are worthless!" At that point, Sarai's temper might have flared up, and she slapped Hagar. This has become Sarai's worst nightmare. "Back in the day," there were songs and choruses that reminded us to wait on God. God may not come when we want Him, but He is always on time.

Children, especially little girls, enjoy playing house. They play with dolls and dress up in adult clothes. Children often fantasize. In 1 Corinthians 13:11, it says, "When I was a child, I spoke as a child, I understood as a child. I thought as a child: but when I became a man, I put away childish things." If we truly love God, we can trust God to put things in the proper perspective.

Adults who "play house" get hurt and often destroy their chances of real happiness in marriage. The common name for a male and female who live together is "shacking" or "shacking up." There is nothing respectful or beautiful about "shacking." Very often, those who settle for such an arrangement become suspicious when they see their roommate or partner talking to someone else.

Some couples who have "played house" are no longer together, even if they did get married for a season. When children are involved and the union is not set up properly, the bond will not be strong enough to keep the couple together. Remember, "when you start out right, you will end up right." When you settle for "playing house" or living together without the sanctity of marriage, you are really living under a curse. God says to you and to me, "If you truly love Me, you will keep My commands," and God's commands are not burdensome or grievous according to 1 John 5:3. Exodus 20:14 tells us not to commit adultery.

Adultery is sex with married people, and unmarried people who have sex are called fornicators (see Deuteronomy 22:22–26). In some cultures, when a young girl moves out of her parent's home and moves in with her "boyfriend" or a man, she is considered to be a prostitute and can never return to the home of her parents. In most cases, marriage does not take place. "Playing house" is not healthy for one's sense of value or self-esteem.

Just suppose you live with someone for a significant period of time, and then there is a breakup. There is an old adage, "When you start out wrong, you end up wrong!" One of those individuals may feel like "used goods," especially if either one gets married. God's way, the "Bible way," is always the best way. Hebrews 13:4 has not changed, "Marriage is honorable and the bed undefiled."

If you are living with the myth of "playing house," get out of that relationship as fast as you can. You are better than that, and you don't have to settle for less than God's best for you. Ask God to forgive you and move on with your life. God is still the god of another chance.

"Playing house" is a dangerous "game" and will only end in heartache. To women everywhere, there is an old saying, "Why buy the cow when you can get the milk free?" If you are at the call of every whim or urge of your roommate or partner without the commitment of marriage, what is the point of getting married? My husband, Reverend Ohanio, had a way of saying, "You have already answered all the questions!" (He was referring to those questions that are usually asked at the wedding ceremony.)

When couples have asked me to perform their wedding ceremony, my affirmative response is based on the fact that I have had the opportunity of giving them some counsel before the ceremony takes place, and I also pray with them.

When the couple has been living together, I suggest that they live apart; if that is not possible, a suggestion is made that they refrain from sex until after the wedding. You might be thinking, *What difference does it make since they are getting married?* There is an old adage that says, "Familiarity breeds contempt."

"Playing house" before the proper wedding robs the couple of excitement and wonder. If, however, they love each other and are committed to the marriage relationship, with the Lord's help, they can be happily married for a lifetime.

What does it mean when a person says, "Come live with me"? What are the circumstances? If it is after an emergency situation, it might be a loving and caring invitation to come and share in the blessings of that home. I often say, "Communication is key!" Before we decide to accept the offer, we must have a clear understanding of the conditions of the offer, and especially the length of time the person is to be at that location. If the invitation has come from a person who lives in an apartment building or apartment complex, can guests stay for any length of time? That would be one of the key questions to be asked. If there is no emergency situation or crisis, the dynamics are very different.

What does it mean when a man or anyone asks, "Will you come and live with me?" What are the ramifications involving such a question? To me, when a man asks me, "Will you come and live with me?" he is showing his "true colors" and not with my best interests in mind. First of all, he is not asking me to become his partner for life, and he is not asking me to marry him. What he is really saying to me is, "Come share my bed with me," and he has no intention of ever marrying me. He may not be committed to marrying anyone. As men sometimes do, he might just be testing me to see how I might respond. Ladies, we can help our men; we can make them more responsible, more accountable, and certainly stronger by saying no!

Some men are accustomed to asking the question involving sexual favors because it is part of their makeup. They may feel that it is expected of them. Saying no to a man is a sign to him that you are different. Etched in my memory is a sermon that I heard many years ago, "You'll live a long time when you learn to say no!"

When someone says to you, "Here is the key to my apartment (or my house)," make sure that you understand the intent. The same holds true when you give your key to someone. There may be great expectations in the giving and receiving of keys. That old adage is still very much alive today, "Why buy the cow when you can get the milk free?" When people have low self-worth or self-esteem (male or female) and do not realize or understand their true value, they may succumb to such an invitation, "Will you come and live with me?" If we give in to such a proposal or proposition, the probability of ever finding our true partner in life will be greatly diminished. Remember, "Familiarity breeds contempt"!

Personally, if a man were to ask me that question, "Will you come and live with me?" That would be like a slap in my face!

Let me back up a little. Could it be that I misunderstood what was said or asked? Could I have heard it wrong? Maybe, just maybe, he might not have meant what I thought I heard or perceived. So let us back up again; clear the mind and ears and ask that the statement or question be repeated. "What did you just ask me?" Way, way "back in the day," I heard this statement, and I have quoted it through the years, "I know you think you understood what you thought I said, but I'm not sure you realize that what you thought you heard is not what I meant." That statement is believed to be anonymous; however, it is still applicable today. All of us must make sure that we understand everything that is said or implied. Communication is still key!

The Glamour Has Gone

I would like for you to meet Paul. Paul is a good-looking guy who doesn't seem to be interested in having a lasting relationship with a woman. He enjoys the "conquest," the "chase." Paul is always well dressed, and he does not mind spending his money. He is health conscious and does not frequent "fast-food" places. Paul is friendly, has great grammar skills, and the average woman who meets Paul will think that he is the "man of her dreams"!

This is how Paul operates, after several dates, and after he gets what he wants, he stops calling. Paul seems to be turned on by the "chase." When a lady says no, Paul thinks that she is playing some game. He thinks that it is just a matter of time, and he will have sex with her, and so the chase begins.

Could it be that something from Paul's past crippled him from enjoying a lasting relationship with someone of the opposite sex? Could it be possible that Paul had been hurt as a child or in another relationship and Paul will not let that happen again?

Paul has just met Susan. Susan is a beautiful twenty-five-year-old, young lady with her own apartment. Paul has had several dates with Susan. They spent what she thought was quality time together. After three months, Paul stopped calling her, and Susan was devastated. She wondered, "What had gone wrong?" She really liked Paul more than any of the others that she had dated. Susan thought that Paul really liked her. After all, they were seeing each other every weekend, and they talked to each other during the week. Susan remembered that she had let her "guard down" and allowed Paul to spend the night with her. There are so many men like Paul. They will do whatever it takes to triumph. Some men will even give an engagement ring, if necessary. I usually advise ladies to wait for the "second ring—the wedding ring." For Paul, the glamour was gone. The conquest, the chase was over, and Paul is now ready to move on to the next conquest.

How many young ladies out there are like Susan? Susan is a Christian who had always been taught that sex outside of marriage is wrong. She had vowed that the first time that she would have sex would be on her wedding night. Susan had let her heart rule instead of her head. There was that "unguarded moment." Perhaps she let Paul kiss her on the lips, and the kiss was too long. Susan was inexperienced, naïve, and vulnerable. When she realized what was happening, it was too late. Susan cries herself to sleep on many nights and wonders if she will ever be able to trust a man again. She really thought Paul cared for her. Paul, however, was only interested in the excitement of the conquest. He proved that her "no" was not really "no"! Susan had misread Paul's kind words and his attention to her on their weekend dates.

Susan, like so many Christian ladies that I have met, are getting tired of being alone and single. They are tired of going out with their girlfriends, tired of going to weddings, anniversaries, and baby showers. To them, the clock is ticking, ticking, ticking! Some years ago, my "spiritual mom" and mentor, Rev. Dr. Mary Watson Stewart of Detroit, Michigan, shared the following remark that was made by a young lady who evidently was a little jealous of another young lady and her upcoming wedding. She made this remark, "I wonder what he sees in her?" Mom Stewart, without hesitation, replied, "Maybe it's what he didn't see!" So often, in today's world, you don't have to use your imagination—it's right there before your eyes.

I would encourage all single people, male or female, to enjoy your singleness. There is nothing wrong with being single. Be single and satisfied. When you are not happy, your countenance and your attitude show. Remember that we are not to be anxious or worried about anything, for God knows what we need.

When you are single, you can decide whether to cook or not to cook. You get to choose where and when to go on vacation. You can spend all your money on you. You are not accountable to a partner. You are free, free, free! The rule is, do not settle for less than God's best for you. Is it really that important to be holding on to someone's arm or going out just to be able to say, "I went out on a date"? Get real! Until God sends the right person for you, be content with who you are, for you are "fearfully and wonderfully made" (Psalm 139:14).

Many of us are just like Paul; we buy an item on sale. We just had to have it until we brought it home. We have not worn it or used it, and after a while, we are ready to give it away or throw it away. If you were to look in your closet, is there anything that you purchased on a whim or you thought that you just had to have? Now that you have the item, you may be wondering, "Why did I ever buy it? I don't even like it." It could be clothing or a game, etc., and you have spent more money than you could afford. Now you have no interest. "The glamour has gone." You may even feel guilty that you purchased it, sale or no sale. Was it really worth what you paid?

Familiarity breeds discontent. This is a fact. All you have to do is look at young children as the holidays approach. Many of them have great expectation of some game, toy, or some other item that they have seen advertised, and they just must have it. The item or items are purchased. Parents and family alike stand in long lines, especially on "Black Friday," just to get that special gift. Once the batteries wear out or the thrill is gone, they are no longer interested. They may not even know where the item is. They are just like Paul—ready to move on to something new or more exciting. That is how sex is outside of marriage; it becomes cheap or devalued.

Sex outside of marriage is called fornication or adultery. "Fornication" is the term used when two people become sexually intimate outside of the marriage bond or covenant. "Adultery" is the word used when married couples have sexual relations outside of their marriage bond. Sexual sins are listed as works of the flesh. (See Galatians 5:19, 21.)

Premarital sex is not God's plan for us. Sex in marriage is ordained by God. The marriage bed is to be "sacred" and respected and enjoyed by both partners. Premarital sex is never the test to show that you really love or care for someone. True love is always willing to wait. My mind goes back to the months before our wedding day. Ohanio could always tell me how many more days until the wedding.

I remember very vividly, before I said, "Yes!" Ohanio emphatically told me, "If you are saying that you are not getting married to anybody for the next two years, I will not be coming over from New York every weekend. I am not saying that I will be seeing anyone else, but I will not come over every week." I did not understand the full impact of his words until some time later.

What Is Love?

The dictionary defines "love" as a noun; it is also a strong or passionate affection for a person (usually) of the opposite sex. Let us put first things first. Before we can honestly love another person, we must first love God. In 1 John 4:7, it says, "Beloved, let us love one another, for love is of God; and everyone who loves is born of God and knows God." Verse 8 further states, "He who does not love does not know God, for God is love." Such love is of a divine nature. "Agape" is the Greek name for such a love as this. This God kind of love is unconditional; it is selfless and self-giving. Romans 5:8 boldly declares, "But God demonstrates His own love toward us, in that while we were still sinners, Christ died for us."

What is love? Chapter 13 of 1 Corinthians is a good measuring rod for any couple contemplating marriage. This chapter teaches us that love suffers long and is kind. Love does not envy. Love does not put on a show. Love is sincere at all times. Love is what it is, genuine! Love is selfless; it is not easily annoyed. Love builds up and thinks on the positive side. Verse 13 emphatically says, "And now abide faith, hope, love, these three, but the greatest of these is love."

I have been given permission to share the "love story" of Marvin and Sandra (Sandy) Johnson. They were our close friends. In fact, Sandra Allen and her sister, Yvonne Allen, were hostesses at our twenty-fifth wedding anniversary. They had our guests to sign the guest book. Marvin and Sandy were married six years later. A few years after their wedding, Sandy realized that inwardly, she was not well. Even though she was ill, she continued to maintain a home and work. She started her own business.

They were a beautiful and devoted couple and desperately wanted to have a child. The doctors gave them no hope. Marvin and Sandy sought the Lord earnestly in prayer, and nothing happened! They believed that nothing was too hard for God. They kept on praying. Sandy often said, "Walk by faith and not by sight!" While in her company, she would say, "If you have faith the size of a mustard seed, that's all the faith you need to get you through." (Have you ever seen a grain of mustard seed? It is like a speck or a dot.)

Guess what? Seventeen years later, their "miracle baby" came! They named her Monica. They held on to a promise. Monica is a well-educated and beautiful young lady. Marvin and Sandy were married for forty-five years. Theirs was a "blissful marriage" and a "happy family"! Some months ago, Sandy's body gave visible evidence that her days here on earth were coming to a close, and hospice came into their home. Marvin set his work schedule to be within five minutes away, if Sandy needed him, or if the hospice called. Marvin called me in March to let me know that Sandy had made her "transition," and Marvin and Monica asked me to do Sandy's eulogy. They both wanted me to custom-make the message to fit Sandy's life. "Love" was the only word that entered my mind, and as I was on my way to the library, the two great poets of the nineteenth century—Elizabeth Barrett Browning and Robert Browning—just stood out in my mind's eye. They were known for their literary skills and their love for each other. Elizabeth wrote a love letter to Robert and Sandy wrote a love letter to Marvin. First, let me share some of the letter written by Elizabeth Barrett Browning, and she also had health issues.

Sonnet 43 (XLIII)
How do I love thee? Let me count the ways

"How do I love thee? Let me count the ways.
I love thee to the depth and breadth and height.
My soul can reach, when feeling out of sight.
–and, if God chooses, I shall but love
thee better after death."

In spite of Sandy's pain and suffering, she remained loving, kind, and selfless. Marvin's last birthday was on February 24, 2014. Knowing that her remaining time was short, Sandy wrote the following letter to her husband, her sweetheart, and her best friend:

> For my darling husband, forty-five years of happiness, God knew and God knows you have made me so happy. I know I have made you happy too. Time has gone by so quickly, and when I look back, I say to myself: fort-five years? Please know you are so loving and devoted. I thank God for all we share and will share if it's His will. Thank you for a life that

has been made bigger and better because of you and God's mercies.

I love you, Marvin Enolls Johnson.

Love,
Your wife—your bride

We are all able to perform the greatest work in the world. That great work is "love." The Apostle John, in his later years, lost his strength and had to be carried to different places. His message was always the same from 1 John 4:7, "Love one another."

When looking for someone to spend the rest of your life with, ask yourself the question, "If I become sick or something devastating or unexpected happens, will my partner remain true to our vows?"

Allow yourself time to observe your "future partner" in a variety of settings. How caring or attentive is he or she to parents or relatives who are sick or in a nursing home? Learning about a person takes time, so take the time. It is your future—your happiness. How much is your "future partner" willing to give so that you may be happy? After much prayer and over a period of time, God will guide you in making the right choice.

- Love is wanting the best for the one you love.
- Love will make sacrifices—not out of duty but out of love.

- Love will overlook faults.
- Love looks for ways to celebrate and affirm the one you love.
- Love will allow you to imagine your "beloved" in an outfit and surprise him or her with it not only on special days but on any day. Every day is special when you are in love.
- Love gave Ohanio and me so many opportunities to look for ways to express our love for and to each other.

Until Death Do Us Part

REFLECTIONS

I will bless the Lord at all times; His praise shall continually be in my mouth. O magnify the Lord with me, and let us exalt His name together. (Psalm 34: 1, 3 NKJV)

Through the gift of memory, I can still capture special moments that Ohanio and I shared during our marriage. There were times when I was getting ready to leave the house and Ohanio would say, "Let me look at you. I don't want anyone laughing at you." (That was a part of his great sense of humor.)

In his preaching and teaching, Ohanio would often remind the ladies about their looks. One of those remarks was "If your hair was in rollers when your husband left for work, don't let him find you in rollers when he comes home from work. Remember, he's looking at pretty women all day long."

There were occasions when we dined out or were on vacation, and I would be concerned about eating the dessert. Ohanio would say, "Honey, go on and eat the dessert. You know what to do when you get home. Anyone who can get into their wedding gown after twenty-five years does not need someone to tell them what to do."

Although our friends Dr. Annabelle and Brother Lloyd Freeland are now with the Lord, we shared many years of wonderful fellowship. They both enjoyed watching us together. At a Christmas party, someone volunteered to get a plate of food for Ohanio. He said, "My wife will fix my plate. She knows what I like. Dr. Ann and I were traveling partners, and some time later, as she and I were sharing thoughts, she gave me an account of the Christmas party. Dr. Ann watched Ohanio as his eyes followed me with pride and admiration when I left the table to get his food. Just a reflection of some memorable moments in our lives.

About the Author

Dr. Mary White Williams is a retired pastor of the African Methodist Episcopal Church and a retired educator. A native of Newark, New Jersey, Dr. Williams has lived and ministered in the inner city most of her tenure.

She is a graduate of Winston-Salem Teachers College, with a BS degree in education, and a graduate of Newark State Teachers College, with an MA degree in special education. Dr. Williams received her educational and theological foundation from the Manhattan Bible Institute and the American Bible College in Chicago, where she received her bachelor and master of theology degrees. In her quest for further knowledge, Dr. Williams continued her education at the International Seminary of Orlando, where she earned her doctorate in theology.

Her grassroots ministry has assisted those whom society has forgotten, by meeting the needs of the current population and culture through the practical training of life skills. The Agape African Methodist Episcopal Church, Emmanuel AME Church, the Mary White Williams Ministries, Inc., and a newsletter that reaches over five hundred homes on a continual basis (established by Dr. Williams) are a few of the areas that have impacted the lives of thousands over her fifty-plus years in active ministry in the United States and abroad.

With her passion for people, Dr. Williams's ministry is not limited. She has provided scholarships over the years that have assisted numerous college-bound individuals. A sought-after preacher, speaker, and teacher, Dr. Williams is very much aware and actively lives her purpose.

Until Death Do Us Part is a testimonial of her life with her husband, the late Pastor Ohanio Williams. Their ministry together spanned over thirty years and was a blessing to countless individuals. This book is an insight to their successful marriage, influential ministry, wise counsel, and an example of what God had ordained: "Until death do us part."

Index

A

Abram, 139
Adam, 42, 81
adultery, 140, 150
AFRO, The, 53
Agape, 72, 155
Allen, Yvonne, 155
AME (African Methodist Episcopal) Church, 18, 42, 163
Amos 3:3, *35*

B

Berns, Augusta, 53
Bethel Bible Institute, 9
Bethel Gospel Church, 61
Bethel Gospel Tabernacle, 9, 23, 27, 61
Bible, 9, 23–24, 29, 35, 38, 61, 72–73, 76–77, 81, 109, 128, 141, 163
Blake, Eustace L., 18, 27
bond, marriage, 74, 150
Boyce, Edward H., 29
Brittain, David, 18
Brown, Lizzie, 14
Browning, Elizabeth Barrett, 157
Browning, Robert, 157
Byrd, Vernon R., 65

C

Caesar, Roderick R., Sr., 9–10, 41, 61
Carpenter, Donald, 23
Central High School, 14
Charlton Street, 11–13
Charlton Street School, 13
Charm Club, 15
children, 5, 11–12, 15, 36, 39, 42, 58, 69, 71, 74, 83, 85, 112, 127–32, 139–40
Christian, 3–4, 16, 18, 25–26, 35, 37–39, 42, 73–74, 77, 83, 101, 130, 148
Christiansted High School, 7
Christie, Eileen, 29
Christie, Richard, 29
cleaving, 67, 69, 71–72, 75, 77
Cleveland Elementary School, 18
Clinton Place, 55–56
Colossians 2:10, *138*
Communication, 97, 99, 103, 142, 144
complement, 40, 120

compliment, 117
contract, marriage, 39
counseling, premarital, 35, 39, 76, 84, 101, 127
covenant, marriage, 75
Cummings, Frank Curtis, 95

D

Deuteronomy 22:13–21, *73*
Deuteronomy 22:22-26, *140*
divorce, 42, 72
Doward, Alma, 6, 60

E

Ebenezer Gospel Tabernacle, 61
Ecclesiastes 1:9-10, *109*
Ecclesiastes 12:10, *102*
education, special, 16, 18–19, 25, 91, 163
Eighteenth Avenue School, 18
Empire Pickle Factory, 13
Ephesians 6:4, *129*
Exodus 20:14, *140*

F

family, 5–7, 11–12, 14–15, 24, 26–27, 29, 36–39, 56, 59–61, 65, 69–70, 83, 85, 121–22, 127–29
1 Corinthians 7:1-5, *75*
1 Corinthians 13:11, *140*
1 Corinthians 13:13, *155*
1 John 4:7, *155*, *158*
1 John 5:3, *140*
1 Samuel 1:1-28, *128*
1 Thessalonians 3:12, *58*
fornication, 73, 150

Foster Gate, 7
Four Star Candy Company, 13
Frederiksted, St. Croix, 3, 6
Freeland, Annabelle, 95
Frost, Robert, 15
  "Stopping by Woods on a Snowy Evening," 15–16

G

Galatians 5:19, 21, *150*
Galatians 6:9, *130*
Genesis 2:18, 21-25, *81*
Genesis 2:23–25, *69*
Genesis 2:24, *69*, *71*, *74*
Genesis 16:1-16, *139*
Glenn (cousin), 61

H

Hagar, 139
Hannah, 127–28
Hebrews 13:4, *37*, *75*, *81*, *141*
Holy Spirit, 28, 37, 39, 73, 76, 111
honesty, 85, 127, 130
honeymoon, 30, 39, 57
Hughes, Frederick, 23
Huntley, Noami, 65
husband, 37, 56–57, 71–72, 75–76, 82, 85, 93, 110, 137, 139, 141, 157, 164

I

intimacy, 44, 57, 71, 73
Isaiah 3:10, *110*
Isaiah 30:21, *77*
Isaiah 50:4, *111*

J

Jackson, Mary, 30
Jamaica, New York, 9, 23, 27
James 1:5, *44, 137*
James 3:5-6, *102*
Jeremiah 29:11-14, *138*
Jeremiah 32:27, *84*
Jesus Christ, 38, 130
Job 28:28, *77*
Johnson, Beatrice, 5
Johnson, Bernice Coppock, 53, 65
Johnson, Marvin, 155–58
Johnson, Monica, 156
Johnson, Sandra "Sandy," 155–57
Johnson, Vera, 23
Joshua 24:15, *35, 38*

L

Lamentations 3:22-23, *77*
Lee, Rosetta, 95
license, marriage, 73
love, 10, 18, 37–38, 57–58, 65–66, 72–74, 76–77, 83–86, 92–93, 117–18, 120, 128–31, 140, 150, 155–59
Luke 6:38, *71*

M

Malachi 3:10, *70*
Manhattan Bible Institute, 23, 29, 163
Manhattan Holy Tabernacle, 29
marriage, 10, 24–27, 35–39, 41–43, 69–70, 72–76, 81–87, 91, 93, 99–102, 127, 137–38, 140–42, 150, 155–56
  successful, 10, 41, 99, 101, 164
Marshall, Hattie, 61
Mary White Williams Ministries, Inc., 93, 120
Matthew 6:33, *91*
Matthew 7:12, *44*
Micah 6:8, *111*
Mickens, Mary, 29–30, 56
Miller, Mathilda, 4–5, 8
Miller, Mildred, 3
Ministers' Wives Alliance, 16
ministry, 61, 93, 95, 120, 129, 131–32
Miriam, 4, 8, 27
Mom Stewart. *See* Stewart, Mary Watson
myth, 135, 137, 141

N

Newark, New Jersey, 11, 14, 16–18, 23, 27–28, 56, 61, 91, 103, 163
Newark State Teachers College, 14, 18, 25, 163
newlyweds, 57, 73–74, 76
New York, 4, 8–9, 23–25, 27–28, 55, 92, 94, 151

P

partner, 35, 39–40, 42–44, 71–74, 76, 82–86, 101, 127, 140–41, 143, 149–50, 158, 162
  future, 158
Paterson, Joseph, 15
Pegram Hall, 14
Philippians 4:6, *44, 82, 130*
playing house, 135, 140–42
Proverbs 3:7, *113*
Proverbs 5:15, *117*

Proverbs 12:4, *93*
Proverbs 14:1, *94*
Proverbs 15:1, *93, 113*
Proverbs 17:17, *44, 110*
Proverbs 18:22, *82*
Proverbs 22:6, *128*
Proverbs 25:11, *93, 102, 117, 131*
Psalm 16:11, *24, 109*
Psalm 19:1, *60*
Psalm 103:1, *86*
Psalm 107, *112*
Psalm 139:14, *17, 111, 149*
Psalm 139:4, *138*
Puerto Rico, 60

R

relationship, 102
    marriage, 39, 142
Romans 5:8, *155*
Rutherford, New Jersey, 19, 58, 91

S

Samuel (prophet), 128
Sarai, 139
2 Timothy 2:15, *17*
sex, 39, 57, 72–75, 83, 85, 140, 142, 147–48, 150, 155
    premarital, 150
Skinner, Arturo, 23, 27–28
SNEA (Student National Education Association), 15
Snead, Phyllis, 65
Soles, Henry, 23
Solomon, 102, 109
South Side High School, 14
Star-Ledger, The, 53

St. Croix, US Virgin Islands, 3, 6, 138
stereotyping, 28
Stewart, Mary Watson, 28–30, 148–49
St. James AME (African Methodist Episcopal) Church, 18, 27, 29, 55
"Stopping by Woods on a Snowy Evening" (Frost, Robert), 15–16
St. Patrick Catholic Church, 6

T

test, blood, 73–74

U

union, marriage, 37–38, 69
Union, New Jersey, 14, 18, 25
Union School, 19, 58
United Pentecostal Council of the Assemblies of God, 42

V

Virgin Islands, 3, 6, 60, 138

W

Washington School, 18–19
Watley, William D., 65
wedding, 27, 29–31, 39–40, 42, 53, 55–58, 65, 69–70, 73, 76, 84–85, 141–42, 148–49, 151, 155–56
Weeks, Eglantine "Dully," 6–7, 61
Weeks, James, 6, 61
Westmoreland, Paul, 77
White, Elaine, 11
White, Henry, Jr., 11
White, Lonzer "Lonnie," 11
White, Nancy Page, 11

White, Roland, 11
White, William, 11,
Whittle, Effie, 23, 25–26, 30
wife, 6, 37, 56, 71–72, 74–76, 81–82, 86, 93–94, 110, 121, 128, 139, 158, 162
Williams, Christian, 3–4
Williams, Mary White, 11, 26, 93, 120, 163
Williams, Ohanio Alexander, 3–10, 23–31, 41–43, 55, 57–61, 76, 82–83, 85–86, 91–95, 99–101, 103, 109–10, 120–21, 130–32, 138
Winston-Salem Teachers College, 14, 163
Women's College, 15

Y

YWCA, 15

Z

Zeta Phi Beta Sorority, 15

Edwards Brothers Malloy
Thorofare, NJ USA
May 28, 2015